A TREATISE ON GOD AS FIRST PRINCIPLE

John Duns Scotus

Table of Contents

A TREATISE ON GOD AS FIRST PRINCIPLE

John Duns Scotus

1.1 May the First Principle of things grant me to believe, to understand and to reveal what may please his majesty and may raise our minds to contemplate him.

1.2 O Lord our God, true teacher that you are, when Moses your servant asked you for your name that he might proclaim it to the children of Israel, you, knowing what the mind of mortals could grasp of you, replied: "I am who am," thus disclosing your blessed name. You are truly what it means to be, you are the whole of what it means to exist. This, if it be possible for me, I should like to know by way of demonstration. Help me then, O Lord, as I investigate how much our natural reason can learn about that true being which you are if we begin with the being which you have predicated of yourself.

1.3 Although being has many properties it would not be irrelevant to consider, it is to the more fruitful source of the essential order that I turn, proceeding according to the following plan. I shall set forth in this first chapter the four divisions of order. From this one can gather how many kinds of essential orders exist.

1.4 For a division to be clear it is necessary (1) that the members resulting from the division be indicated and thus be shown to be contained in what is divided, (2) that the mutually exclusive character of the parts be manifest, and (3) that the classification exhaust the subject matter to be divided. The first requirement will be met in this chapter; the others, in the second. With no attempt at justification, then, in the present chapter I shall simply enumerate the divisions and explain the meaning of the parts.

A TREATISE ON GOD AS FIRST PRINCIPLE

1.5 I do not take essential order, however, in the strict sense as do some who say that what is posterior is ordered whereas what is first or prior transcends order. I understand it rather in its common meaning as a relation which can be affirmed equally of the prior and posterior in regard to each other. In other words I consider prior and posterior to be an adequate division of whatever is ordered, so that we may use the terms order and priority or posteriority interchangeably.

1.6 First Division: In the first place then I say that the primary division of essential order appears to be that of an equivocal term into its equivocates, namely into the order of eminence and the order of dependence.

1.7 In the first, what is eminent is said to be prior whereas what is exceeded in perfection is posterior. Put briefly, whatever in essence is more perfect and noble would be prior in this manner. It was this kind of priority Aristotle had in mind in his proof that act is prior to potency in the ninth book of the Metaphysics where he calls act prior according to substance and form (species). "The things that are posterior in becoming," he declares, "are prior in form and in substantiality."

1.8 In the second type of order, the dependent is said to be posterior whereas that on which it depends is prior. I understand prior here in the same sense as did Aristotle when in the fifth book of the Metaphysics, on the authority of Plato, he shows that the prior according to nature and essence can exist without the posterior, but the reverse is not true. And this I understand as follows. Even though the prior should produce the posterior necessarily and consequently could not exist without it, it would not be because the prior requires the posterior for its own existence, but it is rather the other way about. For even assuming that posterior did not exist, the existence of the prior would not entail a contradiction. But the converse is not true, for the posterior needs the prior. This need we can call dependence, so that we can say that anything which is essentially posterior [in this way] depends necessarily upon what is prior but not vice versa, even should the posterior at times proceed from it necessarily. These could also be called prior and posterior according to substance and species, as were the others above, but to be more precise, let them be called prior and posterior according to dependence.

1.9 Second Division: Leaving the order based on eminence undivided, I subdivide the order of dependence, for either the dependent is something caused and that upon which it depends is its cause, or the dependent and that upon which it depends are both the result of the same cause, the former more remotely, the latter more proximately.

1.10 Patent enough is the meaning of the first member of this second division and the fact that it falls under the heading of an essential order of dependence. For it is clear not only what cause and caused are but also that the two are so related that the caused depends essentially upon the cause and the cause is that upon which it depends as something prior in the sense explained above.

1.11 But the [sense] of the second member of this second division is not so self–evident; neither is it immediately clear just how it fits under the notion of essential dependence. Its meaning is explained as follows. If one and the same cause produces a dual effect, one of which is such that by its nature it could be caused before the other and therefore more immediately [e.g. a subject like mind or matter], whereas the second can be caused only if the first is given [e.g. some quality or modification of the subject such as a state of mind or the shape or form of matter], then I say that the second effect is posterior in the order of essential dependence whereas the more immediate effect of the same cause is prior. Such is the meaning of this member.

1.12 From this I proceed to show secondly that this member pertains to the category of essential dependence. In other words there is an essential dependence of the more remote upon the more proximate effect. First of all, the former cannot exist without the latter. Secondly, the causality of their common cause affects them according to a certain order, and they in turn are ordered to one another essentially in virtue of their respective individual relations to a mutual cause. Thirdly, the latter as such need only be considered the immediate cause of the more proximate effect. If the latter is non–existent, this common cause is regarded as only remotely responsible for the rest of the effects, whereas it is considered to be their proximate cause once the first effect has been caused. Now no effect follows exclusively from a remote cause as such. Consequently the second effect depends on this cause as having given existence to the first effect and therefore this second effect also depends upon the existence of the more proximate effect.

1.13 Third Division: Both parts of this second division are further divided. I will subdivide the second member first because it is in line with what we have just been saying. For a more immediate effect is called prior not only when it proceeds more proximately from the immediate cause of the two effects, but also when the common cause is related more remotely to an effect. Suppose the proximate cause of one of the effects, A [e.g. the state of mind], is in no way a cause of the other effect. B [i.e. the mind itself], but some other prior cause is both B's immediate cause and the remote cause of the other's immediate effect, [Al. In such a case there would still be an essential order based on a priority and posteriority of effect so long as the causality of their common cause is itself related to these effects by an essential order.

1.14 That the second member of this division is an instance of the order of essential dependence is not so evident at first sight, but it may be proved in this fashion. Since each effect is essentially ordered to some common third which is their mutual cause, it follows that these effects are also essentially ordered to one another. Then too, the common cause is only a kind of remote cause of the posterior if the prior effect is not produced. Moreover, the posterior effect cannot exist without the prior.

1.15 Fourth Division: The cause mentioned in the first part of the second division is in turn divided into the famous fourfold classification of final, efficient, material and formal cause, which need no explanation. The posterior correlative to cause is subject to a corresponding division, namely (1) that which is ordered to an end—for the sake of brevity we shall call it finitum; (2) the effect; (3) what is made from matter—we may call it the materiatum; (4) what is given form—we may call it the formatum. The meanings of these divisions I shall skip for the present since I have treated them elsewhere at length and shall subsequently touch on them again as circumstances dictate.

1.16 To sum up the fruits of this chapter, we can say that the essential order is exhaustively divided by breaking it down into six orders. Four of these express a relationship between a cause and that which is caused; another represents an order between two things that are caused (we include here under a single heading the two members of the third division); one is the order between something eminent and what is less perfect.

1.17 Two things remain to be proved before our presentation of these divisions is complete, namely, that the parts of each division are mutually exclusive and that they exhaust the subject matter to be divided. In so far as it is necessary for our purpose, we shall deal with these points in the following chapter, wherein certain necessary propositions of a general nature will be proposed and the interrelations of the aforementioned orders will be studied with a view to discerning any necessary entailments or lack thereof that may exist between them, for all this has a great bearing on what will follow.

2.1 In this chapter we offer arguments for the aforesaid fourfold division of order and for the interrelations that exist between essentially ordered terms.

2.2 When the venerable doctor Augustine, writing about your triune self, declared (in the first book On the Trinity): "Nothing whatever begets itself," you, O Lord our God, were his infallible teacher. Have you not impressed upon us with equal certitude this similar truth? (First conclusion) Nothing whatever is essentially ordered to itself.

2.3 For what is more impossible in an order of eminence than that one and the same thing be essentially greater than itself. As for the other six orders, if dependence be taken in the sense defined above, is there any greater impossibility than that one and the same thing depend essentially upon itself? that it exist without itself?

2.4 This too is in accord with truth: (Second conclusion) In any essential order a circle is impossible.

2.5 For if anything precedes the prior, it also precedes the posterior. Deny this second conclusion and you must admit the opposite of the first. Besides, the same thing will be essentially prior and posterior to one and the same thing, and so be both more perfect and less perfect or be dependent and independent of the latter, which is anything but true. In the first book of the Posterior Analytics Aristotle excluded this circle from demonstrations and it is no less possible in the order of reality.

2.6 As I shall make use of it later, I next present a third conclusion, which like the second is proved from, and sufficiently contained in, the first. (Third conclusion) What is not subsequent to the prior is not subsequent to the posterior.

2.7 This is entailed by what we have affirmed earlier. From this it follows also that whatever does not depend upon the prior does not depend upon the posterior; and further, what is not caused by the prior cause is not caused by the posterior cause, for the latter in the very act of producing its effect depends upon the causality of the prior cause.

5

2.8 Under your guidance, O God, we shall compare the aforesaid six orders with one another beginning with the four orders of cause to what is caused. However, I shall not discuss their various differences nor the adequacy of the division. since both seem to be sufficiently known. For such a discussion could become prolix, and besides it is not necessary for our purpose. In six conclusions I shall compare the aforesaid orders but only as regards their overlap or logical ties on the side of what is caused.

2.9 (Fourth conclusion) What is not ordered to an end is not an effect.

2.10 The first proof is this. There is no effect which does not stem from some proper efficient cause; if something is not ordered to an end, it does not originate with a proper efficient cause; therefore, etc. The major is proved as follows. In no type [of causality] is the incidental first. Aristotle adequately expresses this in the second book of the Physics where he says that intelligence and nature as proper causes are necessarily prior to the incidental causes of spontaneity and chance. But what does not depend upon what comes first does not depend upon what is posterior (from the third conclusion above). I am referring to positive things which alone are properly capable of being effected. The major then is evident. The minor is proved thus: Every proper agent acts for the sake of an end, for it does nothing in vain. Aristotle settles this point as regards nature where it is even less apparent [than it is as regards an intelligent cause]. Consequently, no proper cause effects anything save for the sake of an end.

2.11 A second proof for the main conclusion is this. The end is the first cause in causing, wherefore Avicenna calls it the cause of causes. Reason confirms this, for the end moves metaphorically in so far as it is loved, and this is why the efficient cause gives form to the matter. But it is not in virtue of some other cause's causing that the end as loved moves [the efficient cause]. The end then is essentially the first cause in causing.

2.12 Another proof is this. Aristotle in the fifth book of his Metaphysics shows that the end is a cause for it represents an answer to the question: Because of what? which question calls for a cause. Now since the end provides the first answer, it will be the first cause. That it really does so is evident, for if we ask: Why does something produce an effect? the answer is: Because it loves or intends the end. But if we ask: Why does it love or intend the end? it is no answer to say: Because it produces the effect.

2.13 From the primacy of the end, proved in this threefold way, our main conclusion follows. For according to the third conclusion above, if something is not caused by the prior cause then neither is it caused by the posterior [2.7].

2.14 (Fifth conclusion) What is not an effect is not ordered to an end.

2.15 The proof consists in this that the end is a cause only to the extent that the existence of what is ordered to an end depends upon this end as upon something essentially prior. This is clear since every cause qua cause is prior in this way. Now this situation obtains if, and only if, the end as loved moves the efficient cause to give existence to the effect in question, so that the efficient cause would not give existence if the end were not simultaneously contributing its measure of causality. Hence only what the efficient cause brings into existence for love of the end is caused by the end.

2.16 A corollary follows at this point. One should not fail to mention a false opinion concerning the nature of the end, namely, that the final cause of a thing is its last operation or the object attained through this operation. If one were to think that this as such is the final cause, he would be wrong, because this follows the existence of the thing ordered to the end and the latter's existence is not essentially dependent upon it But it is precisely that for the love of which the efficient cause brings something to be that, as loved, is the final cause of what was made, for it is to the beloved that the latter is ordered. At times, it may well be that the object of the ultimate operation is something loved in this way and therefore it would be the final cause. But it would not be because it is the term of such a nature's operation, but rather because it is loved by that which causes this nature. Nevertheless, it is not without reason that the ultimate operation of a thing or the object attained thereby is at times referred to as an end, for it is ultimate and is in some way the best and as such verifies some of the requirements for a final cause.

2.17 Consequently, Aristotle would not maintain that the Intelligences, while lacking an efficient cause, nevertheless have an end in the proper sense of the term. If he would admit that they had only an end, however, it would be in an improper sense where end is understood as the object of their most perfect operation. Or if he would grant them a proper efficient cause, the latter would not be one which produces movement or change, because the four causes are treated in metaphysics where abstraction is made from any physical considerations concerning them. If he assumes them to be eternal and necessary, he would not admit that the First Being gives the Intelligences being after non−being, at least if "after" is taken in a temporal sense. "After" could only be taken in the sense of posterior in the order of nature, according to Avicenna's explanation of the meaning of creation in the sixth book of his Metaphysics, chapter two. Whether or not there is something incompatible about the idea of a thing being caused necessarily does not affect the point of our argument. For if some efficient cause could cause in a way that is simply necessary, and if some end could move the efficient cause in a necessary manner instead of the way that it does, every effect would still be possible not merely in the sense of being opposed to what is impossible, but also because it is not of itself necessary existence, for it is caused. According to the philosophers, however, it would not be possible in the sense that possible excludes any kind of necessary existence, be it caused or uncaused, for they deny that the separate substances are contingent in this sense.

2.18 Another evident corollary is that the end is the final cause of the effect and not of the efficient cause. Consequently, if an agent is said to act for the sake of an end, it is not the end of the agent but the end of the effect that is referred to.

2.19 (Sixth conclusion) What is not an effect is not made of matter.

2.20 Proof: since matter as such is in contradictory potency to form, it does not actually form itself, but requires something else to actuate its potentialities. And this is none other than the efficient cause of the composite [of matter and form], for to make the composite and to actually form the matter are one and the same thing. The first consequence is clear, for no passive or contradictory potency actualizes itself. And if you say that the form actuates this potency, this is true, but it does so as a formal cause. Before this actual formation takes place, then, matter and form must be regarded as separate, and that which unites them has the character of an efficient cause.

2.21 A second proof of the conclusion is this. In the order of relative priority the efficient cause is next to the final cause and therefore it precedes the material cause. But what does not stem from a prior cause is not caused by a posterior cause. Proof of our first proposition. The causation of the end consists in this that by being loved it moves metaphorically. Now it is only the efficient cause that is moved in this fashion.

2.22 A third proof is this. The composite, being truly one, has some unitary entity which is neither the entity of the matter nor that of the form. Now the primary cause of this unity is not the two entities as such, for if one thing is produced from several it is only because of something which is itself one. Neither is the primary cause the matter or the form taken singly, for each is less than the total entity. Their unity then must stem from an outside cause.

2.23 (Seventh conclusion) What is not made of matter is not formed, and vice versa.

2.24 Proof: What is not made of matter is not composed of essential parts, for in every such composite that is essentially one, there is one part that is potential, because to constitute an essential unity according to the seventh and eighth books of the Metaphysics, a thing must be made of potency and act. Anything that does not possess a potential part as an essential constituent, therefore, is not composed. Consequently, it is not formed, for to be formed means to have form as a constituent part. What was said of matter and form could also be applied in corresponding fashion to subject and accident.

2.25 A confirmation of this proof is to be found in what Aristotle says in the seventh book of the Metaphysics. "If anything were compounded of but one element, that one will be the thing itself." And what is more, such a thing could not be an element according to our first conclusion in this second chapter. By using the topical rule a simili, therefore, we can argue: If anything has but one essential part, then it is just that part. And what is more, the latter is not really a part nor a cause, because of the first conclusion just referred to. Consequently, anything that has one intrinsic cause will also have another which exercises its causal influence along with the first. And so the conclusion we set out to prove becomes clear.

2.26 (Eighth conclusion) What is not caused by extrinsic causes is not caused by intrinsic causes.

2.27 This is sufficiently clear from the four conclusions just mentioned. However, there are special proofs for it. The first is that the causality exercised by extrinsic causes expresses a perfection which does not of necessity entail any imperfection, whereas intrinsic causes of necessity imply imperfection. Consequently, in the act of causing extrinsic causes are prior to intrinsic causes in the sense that the perfect is prior to the imperfect. This in conjunction with the third conclusion entails what we set out to prove.

2.28 The second proof is this that intrinsic causes can themselves be caused in turn by extrinsic causes, and are therefore posterior to them in causing. The antecedent is evident in the case of the form. It is also clear in the case of matter to the extent that the latter is a part. We shall show below that it also holds good for matter itself.

2.29 (Ninth conclusion) The four kinds of causes are essentially ordered in their causation of one and the same thing.

2.30 This is clear enough from the preceding five conclusions. But it seems to be reasonable enough in itself that if something essentially one depends upon more than one cause, some order should prevail so that it does not proceed from them in haphazard fashion. For a plurality of causes which are not related to one another as act and potency or possess no unity of order whatsoever cannot be expected to produce something essentially one. Since the four causes are not constituent parts of a composite of act and potency, how then will they produce the same thing if they do not at least cause together? In so far as they are causing the effect, then, they possess a unity of order. By reason of this order they become a functional unit as regards causation even as many things in the universe become an essential unit through order.

2.31 The type of order that obtains in the case of these various causes should be clear from what was said of the mutual relations of end and efficient cause. (See the second proof of the fourth conclusion and the second of the sixth conclusion. Also look there and in the eighth conclusion to discover how final and efficient causes are related to the other causes.)

2.32 Here I am not much concerned with investigating how the intrinsic causes are ordered to one another as I make little use of them in what follows. As for one being independent of the other, however, it would seem that matter is prior, for the contingent and informing cause seems to depend upon the permanent and informed, since we think of what can be formed before we think of its form. That is how some explain Augustine's remarks in the Confessions regarding the priority of matter to form. And if you ask, according to what order is it prior? I reply: as the more proximate effect of the same remote cause—more proximate, I say according to that order which necessarily obtains inasmuch as the present production of the form [presupposes the matter is produced]. So far as the order of eminence is concerned, however, it is form that is prior [to matter] since it is the more perfect. Though Aristotle assumes this to be evident, when he compares the two in Bk. VII of the Metaphysics, it can be proved from other statements of his about act and potency in Bk. IX of the Metaphysics.

2.33 Keep in mind, however, that it is one thing for causes to be essentially ordered in causing or as regards causation and quite another for the things which are causes to be essentially ordered, as is clear from Avicenna in the sixth book of the Metaphysics, chapter five. For the first is true and has been shown to be such. Otherwise the following propositions would be false: "Because something loves the end, therefore it causes the effect" and "Because it produces the effect, therefore the form informs and the matter functions as material cause"; nevertheless these propositions are commonly admitted. The second, however, is false, for the end is not the cause of the efficient cause; neither is the converse ever true. Ordinarily, however, the efficient cause is not the cause of the matter since it presupposes it.

2.34 Having completed the comparison of the members of the fourth division, I pass on to a brief consideration of the third, since it is clear that the members of this division are mutually exclusive and exhaust what is divided, for (Tenth conclusion) if two effects are compared to the same cause, the latter must be either a proximate or a remote cause.

2.35 As for the second division, I propose two conclusions, the first of which has to do with the distinction of the members. (Eleventh conclusion) If one and the same cause produces two effects, one of which is more immediate than the other, it is not always the case that the more immediate effect is the cause of the more remote effect. Consequently, one effect can be prior to another, but not because it is the cause of the other.

2.36 The antecedent of this conclusion is proved by an example and by reason. The example offered is this. Quantity is an effect more immediate than quality, yet it is not the cause of quality, as is evident if we go through the causes. It is also proved by reason. Look [in 1.131].

2.37 The second conclusion has to do with the adequacy of the division. (Twelfth conclusion) Nothing is essentially dependent except upon a cause or upon a more immediate effect of some cause.

2.38 Here is the proof. If it did depend upon something else, let that something be A and let the dependent be B. Now if A does not exist, neither will B. But it is possible for all the essential causes of B to be present as well as all the effects of these causes which are more immediate than B, while A is still nonexistent, for A [by stipulation] is not included among them. Consequently, B will not exist, even though all its essential causes concur and all the more proximate effects are present. All these essential causes, then, do not suffice as causes, even when the more immediate effects are produced. It is clear that this follows, for once the more proximate effects are present, the causes if they are sufficient can cause the more remote effect.

2.39 If you say the argument does not imply that they cannot cause but merely that they do not, you are missing the point. For if you stipulate A cannot exist, then neither can B. The existence of all the aforesaid causes and their more immediate effects cannot guarantee the existence of A, since A is none of these, neither can it be caused by them. Consequently, neither can B be caused by them. For if one thing is a necessary condition for another to be, then nothing which is powerless to bring about the first can account for the existence of the second.

2.40 Neither is it relevant to object that a natural agent can produce something made of matter without being able to create the matter which is indispensable to its existence, for a natural agent is not the total cause of the composite as would be the case if it could produce the latter even were everything else excluded. The reason I bring up the point is this. Even if I were to assemble all the various kinds of causes B possesses, plus those more immediate effects prerequisite for B, A's existence is not thereby entailed, for A is neither a cause nor is it one of the effects enumerated. Still B can exist only if A does. If this be so, then it follows that the aforesaid combination as a whole cannot produce B and in consequence is not its total cause, which is the very opposite of what we assumed.

2.41 As for the first division, I present two similar conclusions, the first of which is that the members of the division are distinct. (Thirteenth conclusion) If one thing exceeds another, it does not follow that the latter depends essentially on the former. Consequently, the first member of this initial division does not necessarily imply the second.

2.42 Proof of the antecedent: the less noble type is exceeded by the more noble (e.g. the lesser contrary by the greater), but the latter is not the cause of the former as is clear inductively [if we run through the causes]. Neither is one a more immediate effect, since the causality of their common cause is not related to them as to essentially united effects, for if it were, then it could not produce the inferior effect unless it had first produced the superior effect. This is clearly not the case with any cause. For if the inferior contrary is produced by this cause, even if the superior has not been produced by any cause, then it follows that the two contraries are not essentially ordered to any cause. Furthermore, if the one of greater excellence is neither the cause of the other nor a more immediate effect of their common cause, then it follows that what is inferior is not essentially dependent upon everything which excels it. This is clear enough from what has just been shown [2.38].

2.43 Though it be superfluous, I add the converse: (Fourteenth conclusion) It is not the case that every dependent thing is thereby inferior to that upon which it depends.

2.44 It is clear that what is composed of material is much more perfect than the material upon which it depends. Possibly the form depends in a similar way upon matter, as suggested in the ninth conclusion, even though the form is more perfect according to the seventh book of the Metaphysics. In the case of orderly changes, too, what is eventually generated depends upon what went on before, for the anterior developments are the more immediate effects of a common cause. Nevertheless, according to the ninth book of the Metaphysics, the later developments are more perfect.

2.45 To show that this division is adequate, I propose this third generalization well known to Aristotle: (Fifteenth conclusion) Plurality must never be assumed without necessity.

2.46 Since there is no apparent need, then, for assuming any primary essential orders beyond the two already mentioned, they alone are to be assumed. This same general principle also indicates that there are only six essential orders into which the second member is subdivided. This many we have shown, and there is no apparent need for assuming others.

2.47 Having made a general comparison of the members of the first division with one another, I compare in particular the posterior of the first order (viz. that which is excelled) with two special posterior members of the second order (viz. the effect and what is ordered to an end) . Here I propose one conclusion, which is as follows: (Sixteenth conclusion) Everything ordered to an end is excelled.

2.48 Proof for this is found in the fact that the end is better than anything ordered to it. This in turn follows from the fact that it is the end insofar as it is loved that incites the efficient cause to productivity. Let the end be A, the efficient cause B and the effect ordered to an end C. Then we argue in this fashion. A is no worse than B; neither is it equally good; consequently, it must be better. The second part of the antecedent (viz. that it is not equal) follows from this consideration. Whatever the reason might be why A would move an equally excellent B, for the very same reason B could move itself, since it is equally lovable and desirable. And so B could be its own final cause, which is contrary to the initial [conclusion] of this second [chapter]. From this consideration it can also be inferred that A is not worse than B.

2.49 Moreover, according to the second book of the Physics, nature acts for the sake of an end as art would act if it were a natural function. But where products of art are concerned, the knowledge which is the art principle [or premise, if you will], is a knowledge of the end or goal to be achieved, whereas it is the conclusion which has to do with whatever is ordered to the end. Now the premise is truer. Consequently, the end, which includes the truth of the conclusion virtually, is more perfect than the subject of the conclusion.

2.50 You may object that at times voluntary actions are motivated by the love of some inferior good and in such a case the end is not as good as the action performed to obtain it. This is illustrated in every action which is good in itself but evil by reason of the end or purpose for which it was performed, for in this case the action is ordered by the agent to an end inferior to itself. Now my answer to this is that our conclusion holds for those ends which lie in the very nature of things such as is invariably the case with the goals which nature seeks or the aims of a well ordered will. But even the instance of the inordinate will does not really vitiate the conclusion, since in this case we are not dealing with the primary cause of the effect. For even granting that such a will does direct its action to some less perfect end, this action has been ordained by some higher cause for a more perfect purpose, for otherwise, it would not have been ordered, as the proof for the conclusion indicates. But if it has a more perfect end, to the extent it is produced by a higher cause, then it follows that something else is more perfect than it is, and consequently that everything ordered to an end is excelled by some end, even though, perchance, it may not be excelled by the immediate end for love of which some proximate agent produced it.

2.51 There is also another answer which might be given to the objection, viz. that the end which the inordinate agent intends is an end only in a qualified sense. But this is not a happy solution, because the efficiency of the inferior cause is a pure and simple case of efficiency. In other words, it does not effect something simply because it is moved as does a stick, which has no end of its own because it is not an agent on its own, but rather resembles a more immediate effect. If the inordinate will, I say, does not produce its effect in this fashion, then its end is an end in an unqualified sense, since there is some proper end in the case of every proper efficient cause.

3.1 The triple primacy of the First Principle.

3.2 O Lord, our God, you have proclaimed yourself to be the first and last. Teach your servant to show by reason what he holds with faith most certain, that you are the most eminent, the first efficient cause and the last end.

3.3 We would like to select three of the six essential orders referred to earlier, the two of extrinsic causality and the one of eminence and, if you grant us to do so, to demonstrate that in these three orders there is some one nature which is simply first. I say one "nature" advisedly, since in this third chapter these three ways of being first will be shown to characterize not a unique singular or what is but one in number, but a unique essence or nature. Numerical unity, however, will be discussed later.

3.4 (First conclusion) Some nature among beings can produce an effect.

3.5 This is shown to be so because something can be produced and therefore something can be productive. The implication is evident from the nature of correlatives. Proof of the antecedent: (1) Some nature is contingent. It is possible for it to exist after being nonexistent, not of itself, however, or by reason of nothing, for in both these cases a being would exist by reason of what is not a being. Therefore it is producible by another. (2) Some nature too is changeable or mobile, since it can lack some perfection it is able to have. The result of the change then can begin to be and thus be produced.

3.6 In this conclusion, as in some of those which follow, I could argue in terms of the actual thus. Some nature is producing since some nature is produced, because some nature begins to exist, for some nature is contingent and the result of motion. But I prefer to propose conclusions and premises about the possible. For once those about the actual are granted, those about the possible are also conceded, but the reverse is not the case. Also those about the actual are contingent, though evident enough, whereas those about the possible are necessary. The former concern the being as existing whereas the latter can pertain properly to a being considered even in terms of its essentials. The existence of this essence, of which efficiency is now established, will be proved later.

3.7 (Second conclusion) Something able to produce an effect is simply first, that is to say, it neither can be produced by an efficient cause nor does it exercise its efficient causality in virtue of anything other than itself.

3.8 It is proved from the first conclusion that something can produce an effect. Call this producer A. If A is first in the way explained, we have immediately what we seek to prove. If it is not such, then it is a posterior agent either because it can be produced by something else or because it is able to produce its effect only in virtue of some agent other than itself. To deny the negation is to assert the affirmation. Let us assume that this being is not first and call it B. Then we can argue of B as we did of A. Either we go on ad infinitum so that each thing in reference to what precedes it in the series will be second; or we shall reach something that has nothing prior to it. However, an infinity in the ascending order is impossible; hence a primacy is necessary because whatever has nothing prior is not posterior to anything posterior to itself, for the second conclusion of chapter two does away with a circle in causes.

3.9 An objection is raised here on the grounds that those who philosophize admit that an infinity is possible in an ascending order, as they themselves were wont to assume infinite generators of which none is first but each is second to some other, and still they assume no circle in causes. In ruling out this objection I declare that the philosophers did not postulate the possibility of an infinity in causes essentially ordered, but only in causes accidentally ordered, as is evident from Avicenna's Metaphysics, B. VI, chapter five, where he speaks of an infinity of individuals in a species.

3.10 But to show what I have in mind, I will explain what essentially ordered and accidentally ordered causes are. Here recall that it is one thing to speak of incidental causes (causae per accidens) as contrasted with those which are intended to cause a given effect (causae per se) . It is quite another to speak of causes which are ordered to one another essentially or of themselves (per se) and those which are ordered only accidentally (per accidens). For in the first instance, we have merely a one–to–one comparison, [namely] of the cause to that which is caused. A per se cause is one which causes a given effect by reason of its proper nature and not in virtue of something incidental to it. In the second instance, two causes are compared with each other insofar as they are causes of the same thing.

3.11 Per se or essentially ordered causes differ from accidentally ordered causes in three respects. The first difference is that in essentially ordered causes, the second depends upon the first precisely in the act of causing. In accidentally ordered causes this is not the case, although the second may depend upon the first for its existence or in some other way. The second difference is that in essentially ordered causes the causality is of another nature and order, inasmuch as the higher cause is the more perfect, which is not the case with accidentally ordered causes. This second difference is a consequence of the first, since no cause in the exercise of its causality is essentially dependent upon a cause of the same nature as itself, for to produce anything one cause of a given kind suffices. A third difference follows, viz. that all essentially ordered causes are simultaneously required to cause the effect, for otherwise some causality essential to the effect would be wanting. In accidentally ordered causes this simultaneity is not required.

3.12 What we intend to show from this is that an infinity of essentially ordered causes is impossible, and that an infinity of accidentally ordered causes is also impossible unless we admit a terminus in an essentially ordered series. Therefore there is no way in which an infinity in essentially ordered causes is possible. And even if we deny the existence of an essential order, an infinity of causes is still impossible. Consequently in any case there is something able to produce an effect which is simply first. Here three propositions are assumed. For the sake of brevity, call the first A, the second B and the third C.

3.13 The proof of these: first, A is proved. (1) If the totality of essentially ordered causes were caused, it would have to be by a cause which does not belong to the group, otherwise it would be its own cause. The whole series of dependents then is dependent and upon something which is not one of the group. (2) [If this were not so], an infinity of essentially ordered causes would be acting at the same time (a consequence of the third difference mentioned above). Now no philosopher assumes this. (3) Thirdly, to be prior, according to Bk. V of the Metaphysics, a thing must be nearer the beginning. Consequently, where there is no beginning, nothing can be essentially prior to anything else. (4) Fourthly, by reason of the second difference, the higher cause is more perfect in its causality, therefore what is infinitely higher is infinitely more perfect, and hence of infinite perfection in its causing. Therefore it does not cause in virtue of another, because everything of this kind is imperfect in its causality, since it depends upon another to produce its effect. (5) Fifthly, inasmuch as to be able to produce something does not

17

imply any imperfection—a point evident from conclusion eight of chapter two—it follows that this ability can exist in some nature without imperfection. But if every cause depends upon some prior cause, then efficiency would never be found without imperfection. Consequently, an independent power to produce something can exist in some nature and this is simply first. Therefore, such an efficient power is possible and this suffices for now, since we shall prove later from that that it exists in reality. And so A becomes evident from these five arguments.

3.14 Proof of B: If we assume an infinity of accidentally ordered causes, it is clear that these are not concurrent, but one succeeds another so that the second, though it is in some way from the preceding, does not depend upon it for the exercise of its causality. For it is equally effective whether the preceding cause exists or not. A son in turn may beget a child just as well whether his father be dead or alive. But an infinite succession of such causes is impossible unless it exists in virtue of some nature of infinite duration from which the whole succession and every part thereof depends. For no change of form is perpetuated save in virtue of something permanent which is not a part of that succession, since everything of this succession which is in flux is of the same nature. Something essentially prior to the series, then, exists, for everything that is part of the succession depends upon it, and this dependence is of a different order from that by which it depends upon the immediately preceding cause where the latter is a part of the succession. Therefore B is evident.

3.15 Proof of C: From the first conclusion, some nature is able to produce an effect. But if an essential order of agents be denied, then this nature capable of causing does not cause in virtue of some other cause, and even if we assume that in one individual it is caused, nevertheless in some other it will not be caused, and this is what we propose to prove to be true of the first nature. For if we assume that in every individual this nature is caused, then a contradiction follows if we deny the existence of an essential order, since no nature that is caused can be assumed to exist in each individual in such a way that it is included in an accidental order of causes without being at the same time essentially ordered to some other nature. This follows from B.

3.16 (Third conclusion) If what is able to cause effectively is simply first, then it is itself incapable of being caused, since it cannot be produced and is independently able to produce its effects.

3.17 This is clear from the second conclusion, for if such a being could cause only in virtue of something else or if it could be produced, then either a process ad infinitum or a circle in causes would result, or else the series would terminate in some being which cannot be produced and yet independently is able to produce an effect. This latter being I call "first," and from what you grant, it is clear that anything other than this is not first. Furthermore, it follows that if the first cannot be produced, then it has no causes whatsoever, for it cannot be the result of a final cause (from conclusion two of chapter two)—nor of a material cause (from the sixth conclusion of the same)—nor of a formal cause (from the seventh conclusion there). Neither can it be caused by matter and form together (from the eighth conclusion there).

3.18 (Fourth conclusion) A being able to exercise efficient causality which is simply first actually exists, and some nature actually existing is capable of exercising such causality.

3:19 Proof of this: Anything to whose nature it is repugnant to receive existence from something else, exists of itself if it is able to exist at all. To receive existence from something else is repugnant to the very notion of a being which is first in the order of efficiency, as is clear from the third conclusion. And it can exist, as is clear from the second conclusion. Indeed, the fifth argument there which seems to be less conclusive than the others established this much. The other proofs there can be considered in the existential mode—in which case they concern contingent, though manifest facts—or they can be understood of the nature, the quiddity and possibility, in which case the conclusions proceed from necessary premises. From all this it follows that an efficient cause which is first in the unqualified sense of the term can exist of itself, for what does not actually exist of itself is incapable of existing of itself. Otherwise a nonexistent being would cause something to exist; but this is impossible, even apart from the fact that in such a case the thing would be its own cause and hence could not be entirely uncaused. Another way to establish this fourth conclusion would be to argue from the impropriety of a universe that would lack the highest possible degree of being.

3.20 As a corollary of this fourth conclusion, note that not only is such a cause prior to all others, but that it would be contradictory to say that another is prior to it. And insofar as such a cause is first, it exists. This is proved in the same way as was the fourth conclusion. The very notion of such a being implies its inability to be caused. Therefore, if it can exist, owing to the fact that to be is not contradictory to it, then it follows that it can exist of itself and consequently that it does exist of itself.

3.21 (Fifth conclusion) A being unable to be caused is of itself necessarily existent.

3.22 Proof: By excluding every cause of existence other than itself, whether it be intrinsic or extrinsic, we make it impossible for it not to be. Proof: Nothing can be nonexistent unless something either positively or privatively incompatible with it can exist, for one of two contradictories is always true. But nothing can be either positively or privatively incompatible with a being which cannot be caused, because it would be either of itself or from another. Not the first way, for then it would exist of itself—from the fourth conclusion,—so that there would be two incompatible things, and for that reason neither would exist, since you admit that the uncausable is nonexistent because of this incompatible element and vice versa. Neither can the incompatible be from another, because nothing caused has a more intense or potent existence from a cause than an uncausable thing has of itself, since the former is dependent in existing whereas the uncausable is not. Furthermore the possibility of the causable being does not entail its actual existence as is the case with the uncausable. Nothing incompatible with what is already a being can come from a cause unless it receive from that cause a being more intense or powerful than is the being of that which is incompatible with it.

3.23 (Sixth conclusion) It is the characteristic of but one nature to have necessary being of itself.

3.24 This is proved thus: If two natures of themselves could be necessary being, then this necessity of existing would be a common feature. And this they would share by reason of some essential or generic kind of entity in addition to which they would differ by reason of their ultimate actual formalities. Now two inconsistencies follow from this. To begin with, each will be a necessary being first of all through that common nature which is the less actual, rather than through that distinctive nature which is the more actual. For were it necessary being also by reason of its distinctive nature, then it will be necessary being twice over, because that distinguishing nature does not formally include the common nature, even as a [specific] difference does not include the genus. It seems impossible however, that the less actual be the primary reason why something is necessary, and that it is neither primarily nor per se necessary by reason of what is more actual. The second impossibility is that neither of the two would necessarily exist by virtue of that common nature which is presumed to be the primary reason why each is necessary. For that nature is insufficient to account for the existence of either nature, since every nature is what it is by reason of its ultimate formal constituent. But it is precisely what—to the exclusion of all else—accounts for a thing's actual existence, that is the reason for its being necessary. If you say that the common nature suffices for existence apart from the distinguishing natures, then it follows that the common nature of itself exists actually and without any distinguishing features, and therefore cannot be distinguished, since the necessary being already existing is not in potency to being [different kinds of things] in an unqualified sense [in the way] that the generic being in a species is simply that kind of thing.

3.25 Besides, two natures included under a common class are unequal. Proof of this is to be found among the different kinds of things into which a genus is divided. But if the two such natures are unequal, one will be of a more perfect being than the other. Nothing however is more perfect than a being having necessary existence of itself.

3.26 Moreover, if there were two natures having necessary being of themselves, neither would depend upon the other for existence and consequently no essential order would exist between them. One of them, therefore, would not belong to this universe, for there is nothing in the universe which is not related by an essential order to the other beings, for the unity of the universe stems from the order of its parts. Here it is objected that inasmuch as each is related to the parts of the universe through the order of eminence, this suffices for unity. To the contrary: One is not so ordered to the other, for a more perfect existence characterizes the more eminent nature. Nothing however is more perfect than a being having necessary existence of itself. What is more, one of two is not ordered to the parts of the universe, because if the universe is one, then it is characterized by a single order and this obtains where there is but one first. Proof: If you assume there are two first natures, since there is a dual term of reference, the nature next to the first has no unique order or dependence and the same is true of each subsequent nature. And thus through the whole universe there will be two orders, and hence two universes. Or else where will be an order only to one necessary being, but not to the other. If one proceeds reasonably, then, it seems he ought not to postulate anything for no apparent need, or whose entity is not clearly revealed by reason of some order to other things,—for, according to Physics, Bk. I, more than one thing should not be postulated where one suffices. Now we show there is a necessary being in the universe from the uncausable, and this in turn from what is first in causing, and the latter from what is caused. But from these effects there is no apparent necessity for assuming several first causing natures; furthermore, this is impossible, as will be shown later in the fifteenth conclusion of this third chapter. Therefore it is not necessary to assume that there are several things which are uncaused and necessarily exist. With reason, then, they are not postulated.

3.27 Concerning the final cause I propose four conclusions similar to the first four in this chapter about a being able to produce an effect. They are also proved in a similar way. The first of these is this: (Seventh conclusion) Among beings some nature is able to function as final cause.

3.28 Proof: Since something is producible (from the proof of the first conclusion of this chapter), something is able to be ordered to an end. The implication is clear from the fourth conclusion of chapter two. That an essential order is involved is even more evident here than in the case of the efficient cause (from conclusion nine of chapter two).

3.29 (Eighth conclusion) Something able to be an end is simply ultimate, that is to say, it can neither be ordained to something else nor exercise its finality in virtue of something else.

3.30 This is proved by five arguments similar to those advanced for the second conclusion of this third chapter.

3.31 (Ninth conclusion) Such an ultimate end cannot be caused in any way.

3.32 This is proved from the fact that it cannot be ordained for another end; otherwise it would not be ultimate. It follows further that it cannot be caused by an efficient cause (from conclusion four of chapter two and also from what was said above in the proof for the third conclusion of the present chapter).

3.33 (Tenth conclusion) The being which can be an ultimate end actually exists, and that this primacy pertains to some actually existing nature.

3.34 The proof for this is like that used for the fourth conclusion of chapter three. Corollary: It is first to such an extent that it is impossible that anything should be prior to it. This is proved in the same fashion as the corollary to the fourth conclusion above.

3.35 Having set down four conclusions about both orders of extrinsic causality, I submit four like conclusions about the order of eminence, the first of which is this: (Eleventh conclusion) Among beings, there is some nature which excels.

3.36 This is proved from the fact that something is ordered to an end (from conclusion seven of this chapter); therefore it is excelled (from conclusion sixteen of chapter two).

3.37 (Twelfth conclusion) Some eminent nature is simply first in perfection.

3.38 This is clear because we have an essential order. As Aristotle points out in the Metaphysics, Bk. VIII, forms are like numbers. And in such an order, an ultimate nature is to be found. This is proved by the five reasons given above for the second conclusion.

3.39 (Thirteenth conclusion) The supreme nature cannot be caused .

3.40 Proof is found in the fact that it cannot be ordained to an end (from conclusion sixteen of chapter two), and therefore it cannot be caused by an efficient cause (from conclusion four of the same chapter! . The other ways of being caused are excluded as in the proof for the third conclusion of this chapter. An additional proof that the supreme nature cannot be caused by an efficient cause is to be found in the reason given for proposition B, in the proof for the second conclusion of this chapter [DP 3.14]. For whatever can be produced has some cause to which it is essentially ordered.

3.41 (Fourteenth conclusion) The supreme nature is something actually existing

3.42 The proof of this is like that of conclusion four of this chapter. Corollary: It is contradictory that any nature should be more perfect or higher than this. The proof for this is like that for the corollary of the fourth conclusion above.

3.43 (Fifteenth conclusion) In some one and the same actually existing nature, there is the triple primacy in the aforementioned triple order, namely, of efficiency, finality and eminence.

3.44 This fifteenth conclusion comes as the fruit of this chapter. It clearly follows from what has been shown in this way. If to exist necessarily of itself is characteristic of but one nature (from the sixth conclusion of this chapter) and if such existence is proper to whatever possesses a primacy in any of the aforementioned three ways (from the fifth and third conclusions for one primacy and from the fifth and ninth for the second and from the fifth and thirteenth for the third), then each of the aforesaid primacies belongs to that unique nature to which the others belong. For each is actually in some −nature (from conclusions four, ten and fourteen), and they are not split up; therefore they are in one and the same nature. Proof of the minor: Otherwise there would be many necessarily existing natures (from the second proposition of the argument just cited). Our point is also proved from the fact that what is first cannot be caused, for only such is first. But everyone of the aforementioned firsts is uncausable; therefore, etc. Proof of the major: How will a multitude arise of itself?

3.45 This is a very fertile conclusion, containing, as it does, six others virtually. Three of these are about the aforementioned orders considered singly, viz. that at the head of each is one nature. Three more identify the first nature in one order with the first nature in the other orders. And this conclusion which is so fertile has been shown through the sixth conclusion alone, as through a kind of major premise. It is good to express the proper majors for these, if they can be found.

3.46 For the first two conclusions I suggest this simple conclusion as a premise. (Sixteenth conclusion) It is impossible for the same being to depend essentially on two things in such a way that its total dependence terminates with each.

3.47 Proof of this: If for a given causal category one cause is the total cause of something, then it is impossible that another cause of the same category should cause the same thing, for then one and the same thing would be twice caused or neither would be the total cause. In like fashion, one could argue that in such a case something would be caused by an agent which, even if it did not cause the thing in question, would leave the latter caused by it, which is absurd. So too it is impossible for the same thing to depend, by any dependence, on two beings when one of them totally terminates its dependence. For if it still depends upon the other, the first does not sufficiently terminate its dependency. Similarly then it would depend upon something without the existence of which it would still exist, and in the same order of being. But this runs counter to the very notion of dependence.

3.48 Having established this conclusion, I now propose the first ones [virtually] included in the fifteenth conclusion in this fashion: (Seventeenth conclusion) There is but one nature which is first as regards any given type of extrinsic causality.

3.49 Proof: If such a primacy pertains to more than one, then it does so with respect either to the same or to a different set of secondary beings. But the first is not the case (from the sixteenth conclusion just established). What is more, in such a case in every one of the secondary things there would be a twofold dependence of the same type, since where two first beings are involved, there is no single dependence. This consequence, however, is unacceptable. The other way is also out, for if the other first and its secondaries form a distinct set, then they will constitute a distinct universe, because the members of the two sets are neither ordered to each other nor to the same thing. Without unity of order there is no unity to the universe. Yet Aristotle assumes the principal goodness of the universe to consist in its single end. And since there is but one order to one supreme [thing] it is enough for me to speak of this universe alone and not to fabricate another for no reason whatsoever; or rather, for which there are reasons to the contrary.

3.50 We also add some probable proofs. The ascending progression in an essential order is from more to less. Consequently, it terminates with one.

3.51 Again, the higher the cause the more effects does its causality embrace. As one goes higher, then, fewer causes suffice, etc. This proof clarifies the previous one.

3.52 Again, it seems clear enough that the primacy of eminence pertains to one nature, for if two natures cannot be so ordered that one does not excel the other (for in this respect they are like numbers), then it is even more impossible that two different natures should be first to the same degree.

3.53 Then there is this argument about the end: No end would fully satisfy everything other than itself. Since this cannot be the case, the implication is as before.

3.54 What is more, no nature would contain virtually the perfection of every other nature. But without contradicting ourselves, we cannot think that no nature is most perfect.

3.55 As for the other three conclusions there are also special proofs for: (Eighteenth conclusion) That being which is first able to produce an effect is most actual, since it virtually contains all possible actuality. The first end is the best, virtually containing all possible goodness. The first of those beings which can excel is most perfect, containing eminently all possible perfection.

3.56 These three cannot be separated, for if one were in one nature and another in another, it would be impossible for one of them to be simply eminent. These three primacies, then, are seen to express three necessarily concurrent features of the supreme goodness, viz. the highest communicability, amiability and integrity or wholeness. For "good" and "perfect" are the same (from Metaphysics, Bk. V) and "perfect" and "whole" are the same (from Physics, Bk. III). From Bk. I of Ethics, however, it is clear that the good is desirable and from Bk. VI of Avicenna's Metaphysics, that good tends to communicate or give of itself. But nothing perfectly gives of itself unless it does so out of liberality. And this is surely a characteristic of the supreme good, since it expects nothing in return from its giving. And such, according to Avicenna (chapter five of the same book), is the property of one who is liberal.

3.57 (Nineteenth conclusion:) But one existing nature is first in the aforesaid triple way with reference to every other nature, so that any such is, therefore, posterior to it in a threefold way.

3.58 Some petulant objector, while admitting the fifteenth conclusion, could say that besides this nature there are many others which though not first in this [threefold] way, are posterior to this first nature according to some, but not all, of the aforesaid orders. They would be posterior only as regards the order of eminence, or of eminence and finality, but not that of efficiency, as some say Aristotle felt was the case with those intelligences that came after the first, or perhaps with prime matter. Now while this can be refuted from what has been said so far, still it is helpful to explain how.

3.59 In the first place the sixth conclusion disproves this, for if to have necessary existence pertains to [but] one nature and whatever is not posterior as regards any of the three orders is of itself necessary being, then there is but one nature which is not posterior by any kind of posteriority. Consequently every other nature is thus posterior in a threefold way. The second proposition of this argument [i.e. whatever is not posterior is a necessary being] is clear from the third, ninth and thirteenth conclusions of this third chapter (add to each the sixth conclusion of this same chapter).

3.60 Secondly, there are proofs for particular orders. Whatever is neither an end nor ordered to some end, exists in vain. Among beings, [however], nothing exists in vain. Every nature other than the first end, therefore, is ordered to some end, and if to some end, then it is ordered to the first end (from the third conclusion of the second chapter).

There is a similar proof as regards the eminent. Whatever is neither supreme nor excelled by another has no degree of perfection whatsoever, and therefore is nothing. Whatever is not supreme, then, is excelled by something and therefore by what is supreme (from the third conclusion of the second chapter) . 3.61 From these we show what was denied about efficiency [by the petulant objector above, viz. that the secondary intelligences and primary matter are not ordered to a first efficient cause]. Everything is either the first end or is ordered thereto as we have just shown, therefore everything is either the first efficient cause or an effect thereof for the members of the latter disjunct are interchangeable with those of the former as regards posteriority. This is clear from the fourth and fifth conclusion of the second chapter so far as the posterior [portion of the disjuncts are concerned]; as for the prior portion, this is clear from the argument just above.

3.62 A similar proof is that based on the order of eminence. If everything is either supreme or excelled by what is supreme, then everything is either the first efficient cause or an effect, for these members are also interchangeable—from last and second last conclusions of the second chapter and the thirteenth conclusion of this one. What is more, it is quite irrational to assume the existence of some being which has no order [i.e. is essentially unrelated to anything in the universe], as has been shown by the second reason for the sixth conclusion and, to some extent, by the proof for the seventeenth conclusion of this chapter.

3.63 Indeed, O Lord, in wisdom you have made things so ordered that any reasonable intellect may see that every being is ordered. Consequently, it was absurd for the philosophers to deny order of some. From the universal statement "Every being is ordered," then, it follows that not every being is posterior and not every being is prior, since in either case an identical thing would be ordered to itself or else a circle in the ordered would be assumed. Consequently there is some prior being which is not posterior, and is therefore first. And there is some posterior being which is not prior. But nothing exists which is neither prior nor posterior. You are the unique first, and everything besides you comes after you by reason of a threefold order, as I have explained to the best of my ability.

4.1 The simplicity, infinity and intellectuality of the First Being.

A TREATISE ON GOD AS FIRST PRINCIPLE

4.2 O Lord, our God, if you would grant me that favor, I would like to show somehow those perfections which I do not doubt are in your unique and truly first nature. I believe that you are simple, infinite, wise, and endowed with a will. And as I wish to avoid a [vicious] circle in the proofs, I shall begin with certain conclusions about simplicity which can be proved at the outset. The other remarks about simplicity I shall defer until we come to the proper place where they can be proved.

4.3 The first conclusion to be established in this fourth chapter, therefore, is this: (First conclusion) In itself the first nature is simple.

4.4 I have said "in itself," for here I am considering only essential simplicity, which rules out absolutely any composition as to essence. The proof is as follows: since the first nature is not caused (from the third conclusion of chapter three), it lacks the essential parts of matter and form. Neither does it have such diverse perfections, as are so distinct in the thing that one could form a notion of genus and difference from them. Proof of this is to be found in the first argument for conclusion six of the third chapter [3.24]. For either one or the other of those perfections would, properly speaking, be the primary reason why the whole is a necessary being and the remaining perfection would be necessary neither primarily nor of itself—and then, since the latter is essentially included in the whole, the whole will not be a necessary being because it formally includes what is not necessary—or else, if the whole were primarily a necessary being by reason of both realities, then it would be a necessary being twice over and would have primarily two beings neither of which essentially includes the other. Likewise, one would not be the other, for if each is the primary source of necessary existence, then the two will not constitute one thing. For each will be the ultimate actuality and so either no single thing will result from them or else there will be no difference between them and so there will not be two such realities.

4.5 Corollary: The first nature does not fall into a genus. This is plain from the foregoing. It is also proved as follows. The whole of the nature which falls into a genus is expressed by a definition in which what the genus expresses is not entirely the same as what the difference expresses; otherwise there would be useless repetition. Such is not the case with something as simple as the first nature.

4.6. Here an objection is raised: If a thing can be a necessary being only by reason of one, but not the other of two realities in it (for otherwise it would be necessary twice over), then it follows that in a necessary being one can never assume the existence of any realities that are formally distinct. Therefore one could never postulate such a distinction between the essence and relation in a Divine Person. The consequent is false, therefore the first proof is invalid. A similar objection can be raised against the second argument that each will be the ultimate actuality or else one is unnecessary. To this I reply: wherever we have two formally distinct entities, if they are compatible like act and potency or as two realities fit by nature to actuate the same thing, then if one is infinite, it not only can, but does indeed include the other by identity, for otherwise the infinite would be composed, which is disproved by the ninth conclusion of this chapter. But if it be finite, it does not include by identity anything which according to its formal meaning is primarily diverse. For such finite realities are mutually perfectible and can serve as component parts. Consequently, from the assumption that a necessary being consists of two realities neither of which contains the other through identity—the condition required for composition—it follows that one of the two will not be necessary either formally or by identity, or else the whole will be twice necessary. Consequently, both proofs hold. The counter instances about the Divine Person are irrelevant, since the two realities involved are not component parts, but one is the other by identity, since one is infinite. Now if you object: "This is just what I want to say: in a necessary being there is a composition involving two realities, but one is infinite," you contradict yourself on two counts; first, because the infinite is not able to form a component part with the other, since a part is less than the whole; secondly, if you postulate composition, then neither reality is the other through identity. Consequently, both proofs are valid.

4.7 (Second conclusion) Whatever is intrinsic to the supreme nature is such in the highest degree.

4.8 This is proved from the preceding conclusion because any such is identical with that nature because of its simplicity. Since that nature is supreme, anything intrinsic to it is the highest of its kind since it is identical with that nature. Otherwise, if anything intrinsic could be conceived to be surpassed in kind, then the nature with which it is identical could also be conceived to be surpassed in kind.

4.9 (Third conclusion) Every pure perfection is predicated of the supreme nature as being present necessarily and in the highest degree.

4.10 A pure perfection is said to be something which is better in everything than what is not it. This description, however, seems worthless, for if we understand it of affirmation and negation, an affirmation is no better than a denial considered simply as such and as regards any subject able to have what is affirmed or denied. If these latter qualifications are omitted and we claim the description holds for any subject whatsoever, then it is false, for it is not better for wisdom to be in a dog, for nothing which contradicts a thing is something good for it.

[To this objection] I reply: This is a celebrated description and one may explain it in this way. Take "better than what is not it" as referring to anything which is both positive and incompatible [and hence] entails the idea of not being this thing. It is better in this way, I say, in anything—not for anything, but in anything [and] insofar as it itself is concerned, for it is better than the [positive] incompatible feature which prevents it from being present. Briefly, then, one may say that a pure perfection is whatever is absolutely and without qualification better than anything incompatible with it. This is the way the phrase "in everything than what is not it" should be understood, i.e. whatever is not it. For the rest I am not concerned with the description. I accept the first part which is clear, and only add that one should understand "incompatibility" in the sense of denominative predication, since it is commonly treated in this way [i.e. no possible subject could consistently have both predicates simultaneously].

4.11 Interpreting the third conclusion in this way, I prove it as follows: some relationship in terms of being more or less noble exists between a pure perfection and whatever is inconsistent with it. Since by definition it is not excelled by the latter, it must excel the same. Consequently, it is either incompatible with the supreme nature and hence excels it, or else it is consistent with it and can exist there in the highest degree, for thus it is compatible with [this nature], if it is compatible with anything. Now it exists there in the way that is consistent with it. However it does not pertain to the nature as a contingent accident. Therefore either it is identical with it or it is at least a proper attribute. [In either case] we have what we set out to prove, viz. that it necessarily exists in such a nature. I prove that it is not existing there contingently as some incidental accident. For every perfection to which necessity is not repugnant is possessed more perfectly by whatever has it necessarily than by what possesses it only contingently. Necessity however is not repugnant to a pure perfection, for then something incompatible with it would excel it, such as that which is or can be necessary. But nothing can possess a pure perfection more perfectly than the first nature (from the second conclusion of this chapter). Therefore, etc.

4.12 Before taking up what we have to say about infinity and the remaining aspects of simplicity, I deal with the intellect and will, since they are presupposed for what follows. The first such conclusion is this: (Conclusion four) The first efficient [cause] is intelligent and endowed with will.

4.13 The proof is this: The first efficient cause is a per se agent, for according to Physics, Bk. II, every incidental cause is preceded by one that is not incidental but per se. Now every per se agent acts for the sake of an end. From this I draw a double argument: First, that every natural agent, considered precisely as natural, acts of necessity and would act just as it does now even if it had no end but was an independent agent. Therefore, if it acts only because of an end, this is so only because it depends upon an agent which loves the end. Therefore, etc. The second argument is this: If the first agent acts for the sake of an end, then this end moves the first efficient cause either as loved by an act of the will (in which case we have what we set out to prove) or else as loved naturally. But the latter is not the case, for the first agent loves naturally no end other than itself, as matter, for instance, naturally loves form or the heavy object the center [of the earth]. If it did the first agent would be oriented to it as an end, since it is inclined to it by its very nature. But if this end which it loves naturally is nothing other than itself, then we assert nothing more than that the thing is itself. In which case the twofold [causal] aspect would no longer be preserved.

4.14 Likewise, the first efficient cause directs its effect to some end. Therefore it does so either naturally or by consciously loving this end. It is not in the first way, because whatever lacks knowledge can direct something to an end only in virtue of something which does possess knowledge, for "to order ultimately" pertains to wisdom. What is first, however, does not direct in virtue of anything else, just as it does not cause in virtue of anything else.

4.15 Likewise, something causes contingently. Therefore the first cause causes contingently; consequently it causes voluntarily. Proof of the first implication: Every secondary cause causes insofar as it is moved by the first cause. If the first cause moves necessarily then every [other] cause is moved necessarily and everything is necessarily caused. Proof of the second implication: The only source of contingent action is either the will or something accompanied by the will. Every other cause acts by a necessity of its nature and consequently not contingently.

4.16 Objections: [I] To the first implication: Our volition would still be able to cause something contingently. 121 Furthermore, the Philosopher concedes the antecedent [that something is caused contingently] yet denies the consequent so far as God's willing is concerned. For he assumes a contingency in things below which stems from motion. Though motion is caused necessarily insofar as it is uniform, it gives rise to difformity, and so to contingency, by reason of its parts. [3] To the second implication it is objected that it is possible to impede some things in motion and thus the opposite can occur contingently.

4.17 To the first objection, if God is the first efficient cause as regards our will, then the same holds for our will as for other things, for whether God moves our will immediately with necessity or whether he first moves something else necessarily and this latter in turn moves our will with necessity, in any case what is proximate to the will move it necessarily, and thus it would will necessarily and would be necessarily willing. And still another absurdity would follow, viz. that it would cause necessarily what it causes by willing.

4.18 As to the second objection, I do not call everything contingent which is not necessary and which was not always in existence, but only that whose opposite could have occurred at the time that this actually did. That is why I do not say that something is contingent but that something is caused contingently. Now I maintain that the Philosopher could not deny the consequent and still save the antecedent through the expedient of motion, because if the motion as a whole proceeds from its cause in a necessary manner, every single part of it is caused necessarily at the time it occurs. In other words it is inevitable, so that the opposite effect could not possibly be caused at just this moment. Furthermore, whatever is caused by any part of this motion is caused necessarily at the time it occurs and hence it occurs inevitably. Therefore either nothing ever happens contingently, that is, unavoidably, or else contingency is there at the very outset in that even the immediate effects of the first cause are such that it was possible for them not to be caused.

4.19 As for the third objection: If another cause can impede this one, it can do so now in virtue of a higher cause, and so on all the way back to the first cause. If the latter necessarily moves the cause immediately below it, this necessity will prevail throughout the whole chain of causes, right down to the impeding cause which will impede necessarily. At that time, therefore, the other cause could not contingently cause its effect.

4.20 There is a fourth proof for this conclusion. Some evil exists among things. Therefore the first causes things contingently. And the argument proceeds as before. Proof of the implication: An agent acting by a necessity of its nature does the utmost in its power, and therefore it will impart all the perfection it can. If then the first cause acts necessarily and hence every other cause does too (as has just been established), it follows that the whole chain of causes will produce everything it is possible to cause in this effect. Consequently, the latter will lack no perfection which can be put into it by all the causes acting. Nothing it could receive will be wanting, and hence there will be no evil in the effect. The implications are clear, for every perfection it can receive can be produced by some or all of the ordered causes. The last is evident from the definition of evil and the proof holds for a moral fault as for a sin in nature. It doesn't help to say that the matter does not obey, for a powerful agent would conquer disobedience.

4.21 There is a fifth proof for this conclusion, which is based on the fact that a living thing is better than anything not alive, and among living things what has understanding is better than what lacks intelligence.

4.22 Some bring up a sixth proof based on the third conclusion previously established, since they consider it somehow obvious that understanding, will, wisdom and love are pure perfections. However, it is not so clear that these can be inferred to be pure perfections any more than the nature of the first angel can. For if you take wisdom denominatively, it is better than every denominative characteristic that is incompatible with it and still you have not proven that the first being is wise. And if you grant that God is wise, I say that you are begging the question. You can only maintain that, apart from the first being, it is better to be wise than not. In this way the first angel is better than every being, considered denominatively, that is incompatible with it, God excepted. Indeed, the essence of the first angel in the abstract can be better than wisdom in an unqualified sense. You may object that [the nature of the first angel] is inconsistent with many things, and therefore not for everything is it better denominatively than its opposite. I answer that neither is wisdom better for everything; it is inconsistent with many things. You will say: "Wisdom would be best for everything if it could be present, for it would be better for a dog if the dog were wise." I reply: "The same could be said of the first angel. If the angel could be a dog, it would be better to be one; and it would be better for a dog if it could be the first angel." You will object: "No, that would destroy the nature of the dog and consequently it would not be good for the dog." I reply: "In the same way being wise destroys the dog's nature. There is no difference save that the angel destroys as a nature of the genus [viz. substance] whereas wise destroys as a different genus [viz. as a quality]. [Wisdom] is incompatible [with a dog], however, because it requires as its subject a nature which is repugnant [to a dog]. And to whatever the subject is primarily repugnant, to that the property of such will be essentially (though not primarily) repugnant. In ordinary speech about pure perfection there is frequently a failure to make this distinction. What is more, intellectual seems to express the supreme degree of a certain category, substance. How would you conclude from this that it is a pure perfection? The situation is different with the properties of being in general, for they are characteristic of every being either commonly or in disjunction. And how would you refute a contentious individual who claims that the first denominative of any of the supreme genera is a pure perfection? For he would say that any such is better than what is incompatible with it, if taken denominatively, since all things incompatible in this way denominate only their own genus, and it surpasses all of them. If it should be understood as referring to the denominated substances, qua denominated, a similar point could be made. Because if it is a substance that is determined, then this determines the most noble for itself. If not, at least every subject insofar as it is denominated by this, is better than everything insofar as it is denominated by something else incompatible with this.

4.23 (Fifth conclusion) The first [being] in causing causes contingently whatever it causes.

4.24 Proof: It causes contingently whatever it causes immediately (from the third proof of the fourth conclusion above). Consequently, it causes everything in this way, because the necessary does not follow naturally from the contingent nor depend upon it.

4.25 Another argument, from the willing of the end: Nothing is willed necessarily unless it be a necessary condition for whatever is willed about the end. God loves himself as end, and whatever he loves about himself as end will remain even if nothing besides God exists, because what is necessary of itself depends upon no other. Therefore, from the volition of himself, he wills nothing else necessarily. Neither then does he cause necessarily.

4.26 Some objections: [1] The first being's volition of other things is not something other than the first being itself; therefore such volition exists necessarily and consequently it is not contingent. [2] If there is any merit to the aforesaid third proof [4.15] which is the basis for the present argument, then there is no contingency about the causation of any secondary cause unless the first cause be contingent in willing. But just as necessity in the volition of the first cause entails necessity in the causation of the others, so determination in willing by the former would entail determination in the causation of the others. But its determination in willing is eternal. Therefore, every secondary cause is determined before it acts, so that it is not in its power to be determined to the opposite. This is explained further. If it is in the power of this second cause to determine itself to the opposite, then its indetermination in causing is consistent with the determination in the volition of the first cause, since it is not in its power to make the first cause indeterminate, and if indetermination in the second is compatible with determination in the first, then possibility rather than necessity in the second would also seem to be consistent with necessity in the first. Either the third proof is worthless, then, or our will does not seem to be free of itself towards opposites. [31 Again, if the first cause, being determined, in turn determines, then how can any secondary cause move towards something which in some way is the opposite of that towards which the first would move if it were to move, as is the case with our will committing sin? [4] Fourthly, all productivity should be contingent since it depends upon the contingent efficiency of the first [cause]. These are difficult problems, the complete and clear solution to which requires that many things be treated and clarified. Let them be sought in the question I have disputed about God's knowledge of future contingent facts.

4.27 (Sixth conclusion) The first nature's love for itself is identical with its nature.

4.28 I prove this as follows: The causality and causation of the final cause is simply first (from the fourth conclusion of the second chapter). Therefore, the causality of the ultimate end and its causation is completely incapable of being caused in any way. Now the causality of the ultimate end consists in this. By being loved it moves the first efficient cause, which means that the first efficient cause loves the ultimate end. For an object to be loved by a will means the same as for a will to love an object. Hence, the love by which the first efficient cause loves the ultimate end is something completely incapable of being caused. Therefore, it exists necessarily from the fifth conclusion of the third chapter) and consequently is the same as the first nature (from the sixth conclusion of the same; and the deduction is plain in the fifteenth conclusion of the third chapter).

4.29 The conclusion is deduced in another way which comes down to the same thing– If this first love is something other than the first nature itself, it can be caused (from the nineteenth conclusion of the third chapter), and therefore it can be produced (from the fifth conclusion of the second chapter); and that by some per se efficient cause (from the proof of the fourth conclusion of this chapter) and consequently, by someone loving the end (from the same place). Therefore, this first love of itself would be caused by some prior love of an end, which is impossible. Aristotle in his Metaphysics, Bk. XII, proves [God's] knowledge is identical with his nature, for otherwise the latter would not be the best substance, since it is most noble by reason of its knowledge. Now [God] would grow weary if he continued to think, for if his thought were not identical with his substance, the latter would be in potency of contradiction to thinking, and this would produce weariness according to [Aristotle].

4.30 These arguments [from authority] can be established [by reason]. As for the first, every being which is in first act finds its ultimate perfection in its second act, through which it is united to what is best for it. This is true especially if this being is capable of acting in the proper sense of the term and not merely in the sense of producing or fashioning some external object. Now every intellectual being is active in the proper sense of the term and the first nature is an intellectual being, from what we have said; hence its ultimate perfection lies in its second act. But if this act is not the substance itself, the latter will not be the best inasmuch as its ultimate perfection is something other than itself.

4.31 As for the second, only a receptive potency is in potency of contradiction [but this being has no such]; therefore, etc. According to Aristotle, however, this second reason is not a demonstration but only a probable proof. Hence, he prefaces it with "It is reasonable", etc. Consequently, another proof is proposed, based on the identity of the [intellectual] power and its object, viz. [if these are identical], then the act [of knowing] is identical with them. This inference, however, is invalid as is clear from the case of the angel, which knows and loves itself, yet its act is not the same as its substance.

4.32 This conclusion is fruitful in corollaries. [1] For it follows first of all that the will is the same as the first nature, because willing is a function only of the will. Now the will is uncausable; therefore, etc. Furthermore, since the act of the will is conceived as though it were posterior to the will, if the former is identical with that nature, then the latter will be all the more so. [2] It follows secondly that this self–knowledge is identical with that nature, for nothing is loved unless it is known. Therefore this knowledge exists necessarily. [3] Likewise, knowledge, as it were, is more closely connected with that nature than is volition. It follows, then, in the third place that the intellect is the same thing as that nature. We prove this in the same way as we previously established the identity of the will from the act of willing. [4] It follows that whatever is required for this nature to know itself is also identical with the nature, since it exists necessarily in virtue of itself, and is known, as it were, before the [self]–knowledge.

4.33 (Seventh conclusion) No knowledge can be an accident of the first nature.

4.34 Proof: The first nature has been shown to be first in the order of efficiency, and therefore has, of itself and apart from anything else, the ability to produce whatever can be produced, at least insofar as it is the first cause of that which can be produced. But without a knowledge of the latter, the first nature would be unable to produce what can be produced. Hence, the knowledge of any of these other beings is not something distinct from its own nature. Proof of the last assumption: Nothing can cause an effect except by willing it for the sake of an end. Otherwise it would not be a per se agent, since it would not be acting for an end. But before anything can be willed for the sake of an end, it must be known. Hence, before we can even conceive of the first being as willing or causing A, we must conceive of it as knowing A, for without such knowledge the first cause would not be properly a cause. And the same holds true of everything else it could produce.

4.35 Moreover, all the acts of knowledge of any given intellect are related in the same way to that intellect, so that either all are accidents or all are of the essence of that intellect. This is clear as regards all created intellects, all of which seem to be of the same kind of perfection. Therefore, if some of the acts are received by the intellect, all the acts are, and if one of them is an accident, the remainder are likewise. But from the preceding conclusion, the self–knowledge of the first being cannot be an accident; therefore, none of its knowledge is such.

4.36 Furthermore, if some act of knowledge can be an accident, it will be received by the intellect as by its subject. In such a case, however, the act of knowledge which is identical with the intellect and is the more perfect of the two acts of knowledge, would itself be the recipient of the less perfect.

4.37 Furthermore, the same act of knowledge can embrace several interrelated objects, and the more perfect this act is, the greater can be the number of objects. Consequently, an act that is so completely perfect that it would be impossible to have anything more perfect, will embrace all that can be known. Now the understanding of the first being is of such perfection (from the second conclusion of this chapter: therefore there is but one act for all that can be known. Now from what has just been said, self–knowledge is identical with its very being. The same conclusion I wish to be understood of the act of volition.

4.38 It is also argued that this intellect is nothing more than a certain kind of knowing; but this intellect is the same for all things so that it cannot differ for different objects. Therefore, neither is the act of understanding different. Hence, one act of understanding suffices for all objects. I reply: to argue in all cases from the identity of things among themselves to their identity with relation to a third object distinct from both is to commit the fallacy of accident. To illustrate: just because an act of understanding is identified with the act of willing, it does not follow that whatever is known by the act of knowledge is also loved by the will. It follows only that there is an act of volition and that it is indeed related to the same [object though not by a relation of love, but] because it [happens to be identified with what] is also knowledge of the same. The inference can only be made in disjunction, but not in conjunction, since the two are only incidentally related.

4.39 Another argument advanced is that inasmuch as the first being's act of self–knowledge is identical with itself, its intellect has but one coeternal and completely adequate act, and therefore it can have no other. But this inference is invalid. Consider, for instance, a beatified individual who has an intellectual vision of God and as well as of others things. And even if he sees God according to the utmost of his ability, as we assume was the case with the soul of Christ, he is still able to see something else.

4.40 Still another argument employed is this. Since this intellect is identified with the most perfect knowledge possible [viz. knowledge of the supreme nature itself], it also possesses all other knowledge. I reply that this does not follow, for this other lesser knowledge could be caused, and therefore it could be different from the most perfect self–knowledge, which is uncaused.

4.41 (Eighth conclusion) The intellect of the first being knows everything else that can be known with a knowledge that is eternal, is distinct, is actual, is necessary and is prior by nature to the existence of these things in themselves.

4.42 The first part is proved as follows: To be able to know actually and distinctly each and every other thing that can be known is something that pertains to the perfection of knowledge. Indeed, the very notion of an intellect makes it necessary to assume the possibility of such knowledge, for every intellect (as I have established elsewhere) has to do in general with all being. The intellect of the first being, however, can have no knowledge that is not one with itself (from the preceding conclusion). Therefore, it knows everything intelligible actually and distinctly. And this knowledge is identified with it.

4.43 Another argument for this first part is that the perfect artist has a distinct knowledge of everything that is to be accomplished before it is done, for otherwise he would not act perfectly, since knowledge is the norm that guides him. Consequently, God by himself has a distinct, actual (or at least habitual) knowledge of all that can be produced and this knowledge is prior to the things. Against this the objection is raised that a universal art suffices to produce singular things.

4.44 The second part about the priority of the knowledge is proved in this way. Whatever is identical with this being, exists necessarily (from the fifth conclusion of the third chapter and the first conclusion of the fourth chapter). The existence of other intelligible things is not a necessary existence (from the sixth conclusion of the third chapter) . A being that is necessary of itself is prior by nature to everything that does not necessarily exist.

4.45 Another proof: The existence of every other thing is dependent upon this as a cause (from the nineteenth conclusion of the third chapter) and since it is the cause of some such being, a knowledge of the same by the cause is also required. Therefore, this cognition is prior by nature to the existence of the thing known.

4.46 Oh the depths of the riches of your wisdom and of your knowledge, O God, by which you comprehend everything that can be known! Could you not enable my puny intellect to infer (Ninth conclusion) that you are infinite and incomprehensible by what is finite?

4.47 I shall try now to establish this most fertile conclusion, which if it had been proved of you at the outset, would have made obvious so many of the conclusions we have mentioned so far. I shall first try to prove your infinity, if you please, from what has already been said about your intellect. And I shall then bring up other arguments to see whether or not they entail the conclusion we propose to prove.

4.48 [a. The First Way] O Lord God, are not the things that can be known infinite in number and are they not all known actually by an intellect which knows all things? Therefore, that intellect is infinite which, at one and the same moment, has actual knowledge of all these things. Our God, yours is such an intellect (from the eighth conclusion just above). The nature that is identical with it then is also infinite.—I show the antecedent and consequence of this enthymeme. The antecedent: Things potentially infinite in number (i.e. things, which if taken one at a time are endless) become actually infinite if they exist simultaneously. Now what can be known is of such a nature so far as a created intellectual is concerned, as is sufficiently clear. Now all that the created intellect knows successively, your intellect knows actually at one and the same time. There, then, the actually infinite is known. I prove the major of this syllogism, although it seems evident enough. Consider these potentially infinite things as a whole. If they exist all at once, they are either actually infinite or actually finite. If finite, then if we take one after the other, eventually we shall actually know them all. But if we cannot actually know them all in this way, they will be actually infinite if known simultaneously. The consequence of this enthymeme I prove as follows. Whenever a greater number requires or implies greater perfection than does a smaller one, numerical infinity implies infinite perfection. For example, greater motive power is required to carry ten things than to carry five. Therefore, an infinite motive power is needed to carry an infinity of such things. Now in the point at issue, since the ability to know two things distinctly implies a greater perfection of intellect than the ability to know only one, what we propose to prove follows. This last I prove to be so because the intellect must apply itself and concentrate if it is to understand the intelligible distinctly. If then it can apply itself to more than one, it is not limited to any one of them and if it can apply itself to an infinity of such it is completely unlimited.

4.49 This last point I prove in a similar way—at least as regards the act of understanding; and from this our proposed conclusion about the intellect follows. Since to know A is one perfection and to know B also is another, it follows that A and B as two equally distinct objects will never be known by one and the same act of knowledge unless the latter includes the perfection of the two acts. The same holds for three objects, and so on.

4.50 [Objections] [1] It will be claimed that a plurality of things does not imply any greater perfection where the reason for knowing them is the same. [2] Another point, the argument about the act of understanding [4.49] holds only where the several acts would be apt to have distinct formal perfections. Such, however, would be the acts of understanding diverse species of things. Now there is not an infinite number of such intelligibles, as there is of individuals. But where the acts of knowledge concern individuals, which do not differ as to their formal perfection, then no greater perfection is implied by the fact that the acts concern more than one such.—Against the first: The same argument holds for the reason for knowing as for the intellect and its act, viz. that greater perfection is implied where the reason has to do with more than one thing, because it must needs include in an eminent way the perfections of all the proper reasons for knowing, each of which has some perfection by virtue of what it properly is. An infinity of such then entails infinite perfection.—Against the second: Individuals are only imperfectly understood under a universal aspect, since (as I have shown in the question on individuation) they are not known according to all of the positive entity in them. Consequently, an intellect, understanding each individual in all of its positive intelligibility, has knowledge of distinct positive entities where several individuals are concerned, and greater perfection is required of the act of knowledge than where one individual is concerned. For the knowledge of any absolute positive entity insofar as it is just that thing is some perfection; otherwise, if such knowledge were absent, neither the intellect nor its act of knowledge would be any less perfect, and hence, there would be no cause to assume such knowledge in the divine intellect. But this runs counter to the eighth conclusion. What is more, an infinity of specifically distinct intelligibles can be inferred from numbers and figures. This is confirmed by Augustine in Bk. XII, chapter eight, of the City of God.

4.51 [b. The Second Way] I show what I propose to prove in this second way. Suppose a secondary cause can add some perfection to the causality of the first cause, even when the latter acts to the utmost of its power. In such a case, if the first cause were to act alone, its effectiveness would seem to be less perfect than that of the two causes together. Therefore, if something which a secondary cause can produce together with the first cause can be done much more perfectly by the first cause alone, the secondary cause adds no perfection to the first. But any finite thing gains in perfection by the addition of something else. Hence a first cause whose causality cannot be perfected is infinite. To apply this to the question at issue: Knowledge of any object is by its very nature apt to be engendered by that object as its proximate cause, and this is especially true of [intuitive knowledge or] vision. Therefore, if some intellect possesses such knowledge without any action on the part of the object known, but solely in virtue of some prior object which by nature is a higher cause of such knowledge, it follows that the higher object is infinite as to cognoscibility, because the lower object adds nothing to it in the way of cognoscibility. Now, the supreme nature is such a superior object, since in the absence of all other objects by the mere fact that it is present to the intellect of the first being, it Fives to that intellect not only a knowledge of every object without exception (from the eighth conclusion of this chapter) but a most perfect knowledge of the same (from the second conclusion of the same). Therefore, nothing else that can be known adds anything to this nature in the way of cognoscibility. As something intelligible, then, it is infinite. Therefore, its entity is also infinite, for a thing is only knowable to the extent that it has entity.

4.52 Here it is objected: [1] Were such the case, then no second cause, being finite, could ever produce a knowledge of the effect that is as perfect as that which the effect is able to produce of itself. Now this is false because knowledge of a thing through its cause is more Perfect than a knowledge of the same through the thing itself without the cause. [2] Also, all that seems to follow from the fact that the first cause produces just as perfectly without as with the second is that it possesses the perfection of the second more perfectly than does the second itself. But this does not seem to imply infinity, for a finite Perfection could still surpass the second cause in perfection. [3] Also, even supposing nothing is added to the causation of the first cause when it acts according to the utmost of its ability, how does this prove that nothing is added in being? Suppose that in illuminating a medium, our sun would cause as much light as the medium could receive. The addition of another sun would add nothing to the causation of the first but it would add to it in being, since there would be another sun. Similarly, from the presence of the first nature as object there is as much knowledge in the intellect of the first being as can be there. Consequently, the reason a second cause adds nothing in causing is that it is not able to act upon an intellect that is fully actualized, even as a second sun would not be able to act upon the medium. Now if this suffices to prove that it adds nothing in being, then it seems you could argue in similar fashion that the earth adds nothing in being to the sun, because it adds nothing to causing light in the medium.

4.53 I reply to the first objection: Unless we first have a simple idea of the thing in itself, we shall never infer anything about it scientifically [i.e. by way of demonstration]. When by scientific knowledge, then, we know about an effect through its cause, the latter does not produce such simple knowledge of the effect as the latter by nature is able to produce of itself, for—as Augustine puts it in the last chapter of Bk. IX, On the Trinity—"Knowledge is born of the knower and the known." Or if the cause would produce some form of simple knowledge, it would not be that which we call intuitive, about which I have said a great deal elsewhere. Over and above all cognition through causes, then, we look for such knowledge as only the object itself can produce in us. Now if God has intuitive knowledge of a stone, which in no way is caused by the latter, it must needs be that the stone in virtue of what it is able to make known, adds nothing whatsoever to what can be known by reason of the first being's essence through which the stone is known intuitively. When you argue, then, that no finite cause produces perfect knowledge of an effect, I grant it does not produce the most perfect knowledge possible even for us. When you claim that cognition through a cause is more perfect, I say you must include also such simple [i.e. intuitive] knowledge as the effect can cause of itself. Complex cognition is the result of a joint knowledge of cause and effect. Now it is true that what results from the first cause and second together is more perfect than what results from the second alone.—To the contrary: The first finite cause by itself can produce a more perfect effect than can the second alone. Now the second can produce a vision [or intuitive cognition] of itself, hence the first can also produce this alone. I reply: True, the first cause alone can produce something (for example, a vision of itself) which is a more perfect effect than the second can produce alone. But it is not able to cause more perfectly that precise effect which the second by nature was designed to produce either as a secondary cause or rather as a primary cause so far as all other finite causes are concerned. For in causing such cognition [e.g. an intuition of itself] the second cause seems to be only accidentally ordered to any prior finite cause, for such knowledge was not destined by nature to be produced by any finite cause above it. Hence, the vision would exist, even if the thing seen were uncaused by such a higher cause, or if it existed and the intellect existed without the coexistence of any prior finite cause.

4.54 Reply to the second objection: Although the prior first cause contains in a more excellent way the whole perfection of the second in causing, and to that extent surpasses the second which has this perfection only formally, still it is more excellent, even as regards causation, to possess this perfection both formally and eminently than to possess it only eminently. To state it in universal terms, when the formal possession of any perfection adds to the eminent possession of the same, then together they are more excellent than either taken singly. Such addition is possible whenever the higher is something finite, since the finite becomes greater by a finite addition. Were such not the case the universe as a whole would not be more perfect than the first caused nature, which some assume to contain in a more excellent way the perfection of everything below it. But I have denied this above (in the last conclusion of the second chapter).

4.55 Reply to the third: Suppose we are dealing with a perfection which, where causable, either [a] is destined by nature to be produced solely by something which is formally such, something which functions as a kind of primary cause only accidentally ordered to any prior finite causes, or [b] is causable by other finite causes only with the cooperation of something having such perfection formally. A perfection of this sort cannot be given existence by a power whose efficacy is not increased by the addition of anything formally such, unless that power be infinite. Hence, the argument used above [4.51] is valid, for if anything could be added to that power, then such would be the nature of its peculiar causality that something is lacking as regards the perfection [to be produced]. Consequently it depends either upon something which formally possesses this perfection or upon some other power whose efficacy is not augmented by the addition of something formally possessing such a perfection. Since the causality proper to this latter kind of power is rooted in its formal being, it follows further that no addition can be made to its being either. If it could, then the first being would lack that peculiar causality which the other has by reason of its formal nature, and consequently the first would not of itself possess that more excellent being whose nature it is to be caused by something which has that being as such. The example of the sun, it is clear, proves nothing, for if it were within the province of the first sun as such to cause anything, the latter would not only not be caused by the other sun, but this second sun would not even have such a thing in itself without the first sun. I don't care then to what recipient of the effect you refer; if one sun adds anything to the other, be it in causing or also in being, I say in brief, what is added is not that kind of thing that needs to be caused by something possessing such a quality formally—"needs to be," I say, to the extent that it cannot be caused in any other way, nor can it exist uncaused in a more perfect way than it exists as caused, except in the power of something to which anything formally such adds nothing by way of either causality or being. The example of the earth also proves nothing, since light was not made to depend upon it as upon some cause.

4.56 [c. The Third Way] I show our conclusion, thirdly, as follows: No finite perfection of the same formal nature as an accidental perfection is substantial; our act of understanding is an accident, since it is essentially a quality. No finite act of understanding, therefore, is a substance. But the act of understanding of the first being is a substance (from the fifth, sixth and seventh conclusions of this chapter). Proof of the major: Things which agree in that formal reason from which the specific difference is derived, agree also in their genus, if both formal perfections are finite; for such a finite difference tends to delimit the same genus in whatever it may be. Now such is not the case where the difference in one is finite, but infinite in the other; for in such a situation, though there is some measure of agreement as regards the formal reason, still the latter, where it is finite, tends to delimit a genus, and consequently whatever is constituted by such a difference will be in a genus. Where the difference is finite, however, it can delimit nothing. Consequently, a thing of this sort does not fall under a genus.

4.57 It is in this way that I interpret the saying that species, but not genus, is used of the divine in a transferred sense, for species bespeaks perfection whereas genus does not. This characterization, however, entails a contradiction if it be understood of the species as a whole, for the genus is included in the species as a part of its essential meaning. Consequently the dictum should be referred to the species by reason of the difference which does imply perfection, whereas the genus does not. Surely it is possible to do this, since neither the genus nor the difference as such include each other. But even the difference cannot be transferred, qua difference, since as such it is finite and necessarily puts a thing into a genus. What is transferred then is the absolute sense of a difference, which when taken absolutely reveals an indifference to both infinite and finite. "Finite" and "infinite" indicate the measure of an entity's perfection even as do "more" and "less" as regards whiteness.

4.58 Some of the things said here, I know, contradict certain views which I have not bothered to refute at this point, as there will be a place for that elsewhere.

4.59 A somewhat similar, or converse, version of this third proof could be set up as follows. No finite substance is ever the same thing as its perfection which by definition is accidental whenever it is finite. The first substance, [however], is the same as its intellection. [Therefore,] etc.—And then one can add the major of the third reason, [viz.] no finite perfection of the same formal nature as an accidental perfection is substantial, or is the same as the substance, for genera are primarily diverse [i.e. they fall under no common genus] and what is an accident to one is a substance to none. Therefore, an act of understanding is never identified with any substance which falls into the category of that name. If this [first substance] were finite, it would be in such a state [i.e. its understanding would not be the same as its substance]. If this is not so, then we have what we set out to prove, [viz. it is not finite but infinite].

4.60 [d. The Fourth Way] In line with this, I submit a fourth reason. Every finite substance is in a genus, but not the first nature (from the first conclusion of this chapter); therefore, etc. The major is evident, since every finite substance, while agreeing with other kinds by reason of the common concept of substance, is also formally distinguished from them, as is clear. The distinguishing feature is in some way identified with the entity of the substance, but is not completely identical since the formal meanings of the two are primarily diverse and neither is infinite. Consequently, neither includes the other by way of identity; hence, if one thing results from them, its unity is like that of act and potency, or of a limitation and what is limited. In other words, we have a genus and a difference, and therefore a species.

4.61 The same point can be put briefly as follows: Everything really agreeing, yet really differing, agrees and differs by a reality which is not formally the same. But unless one of the two be infinite, they are not identified with each other. But where neither is the other by way of identity, we have tellect {yep that's right}, the fourth grounded in the simplicity of the essence) composition. Therefore everything essentially agreeing, yet essentially differing, is either a composite of formally distinct realities or else it is infinite. Everything existing per se agrees and differs in this fashion. Hence if it is altogether simple, it follows that it will also be infinite.

4.62 By these four ways (three with their basis in the in {yep} God's infinity, it seems, can be proved.

4.63 [e. The Fifth Way] There appears to be a fifth way, that of eminence. According to this I argue that it is incompatible with the idea of a most perfect being that anything should excel it in perfection (from the corollary to the fourth conclusion of the third chapter) . Now there is nothing incompatible about a finite thing being excelled in perfection; therefore, etc. The minor is proved from this, that to be infinite is not incompatible with being; but the infinite is greater than any finite being. Another formulation of the same is this. That to which intensive infinity is not repugnant is not all perfect unless it be infinite, for if it is finite, it can be surpassed, since infinity is not repugnant to it. But infinity is not repugnant to being, therefore the most perfect being is infinite.

4.64 The minor of this proof, which was used in the previous argument, [1] cannot, it seems, be proven a priori. For, just as contradictories by their very nature contradict each other and their opposition cannot be made manifest by anything more evident, so also these terms [viz. "being" and "infinite"] by their very nature are not repugnant to each other. Neither does there seem to be any way of proving this except by explaining the meaning of the notions themselves. "Being" cannot be explained by anything better known than itself. "Infinite" we understand by means of finite. I explain "infinite" in a popular definition as follows: The infinite is that which exceeds the finite, not exactly by reason of any finite measure, but in excess of any measure that could be assigned.—[2] The following persuasive argument can be given for what we intend to prove. Just as everything is assumed to be possible if its impossibility is not apparent, so also all things are assumed to be compatible if their incompatibility is not manifest. Now there is no incompatibility apparent here, for it is not of the nature of being to be finite; nor does finite appear to be an attribute coextensive with being. But if they were mutually repugnant, it would be for one or the other of these reasons. The coextensive attributes which being possesses seem to be sufficiently evident.—[3] A third persuasive argument is this. Infinite in its own way is not opposed to quantity (that is, where parts are taken successively); therefore, neither is infinity, in its own way, opposed to entity (that is, where perfection exists simultaneously) .—[4] If the quantity characteristic of power is simply more perfect than that characteristic of mass, why is it possible to have an infinity [of parts] in mass and not an infinite power? And if an infinite power is possible, then it actually exists (from the fourth conclusion of the third chapter).—[5] The intellect, whose object is being, finds nothing repugnant about the notion of something infinite. Indeed, the infinite seems to be the most perfect thing we can know. Now if tonal discord so easily displeases the ear, it would be strange if some intellect did not clearly perceive the contradiction between infinite and its first object [viz. being] if such existed. For if the disagreeable becomes offensive as soon as it is perceived, why is it that no intellect naturally shrinks from infinite being as it would from something out of harmony with, and even destructive of, its first object?

4.65 In the same way Anselm's argument about the highest thing conceivable can be touched up. His description must be understood in this way. God is a being conceived without contradiction who is so great that it would be a contradiction if a greater being could be conceived. For anything, the thought of which includes a contradiction, is said to be inconceivable, and so it is. For it includes two conceivable notions so opposed to each other that they cannot in any way be fused into a single conceivable object, since neither determines the other. It follows that there is in reality such a greatest conceivable object, as God is described to be. [This is proved] first of its essential being, for in such an object the intellect is fully satisfied. Therefore, in it the primary object of the intellect, viz. being, is verified and this in the highest degree. Next this is established of its existential being. The highest conceivable object is not one which is merely in the intellect of the thinker, for then it both could exist, because as something possible it is conceivable, and yet could not exist, because the idea of existing in virtue of something else is repugnant to its very nature (from the third conclusion and fourth conclusion of the third chapter) . Therefore, what exists in reality is conceivably greater than what exists only in the intellect. This is not to be understood, however, in the sense that something conceived, if it actually exists, is, by the fact of existing, conceivable to any greater extent. What it means is merely that for anything which exists solely in the intellect there is some greater conceivable object which exists in reality.—Or the argument could be retouched in this way. A greater conceivable object is one which exists, that is to say, such an object is knowable in a more perfect way because it is visible [or knowable by intuitive cognition]. What does not exist either in itself or in something more noble to which it adds nothing, is not capable of being intuited. Not what can be seen or intuited is knowable in a more perfect way than something which cannot be intuited, but known only abstractively. Therefore the most perfect thing that can be known exists.

4.66 [f. The Sixth Way] A sixth way to the proposed conclusion, based on the idea of an end, is this. Our will can always love and seek something greater than any finite end, even as our intellect is able to know more. And there seems to be a natural inclination to love supremely an infinite good. For this is the sign of the free will's natural inclination for anything that, spontaneously, and without the aid of any habit, it loves this thing readily and with delight. And it seems that in this way we experience a love for the infinite good. Indeed it seems that the will is not satisfied with anything else. If infinite good were really opposed to its natural object, why does not the will by nature hate such a good, just as it naturally hates non-existence?

4.67 [g. The Seventh Way] The Philosopher treats of the seventh way from efficient causality in Physics, Bk. VIII and his Metaphysics, Bk. XII, where he argues that the first being has infinite power, because it moves with an endless movement. The argument can be retouched so far as the antecedent goes in this way. The desired conclusion follows equally well from the fact that the first being can cause such motion as it would if it actually did so; for in either case the actual existence of the cause would be required. As for the consequence: If it moves with an infinite movement of itself and not in virtue of another, then it has not received such power of movement from another. Hence, it has in its power at one and the same time the totality of its effect, because it has this power independently. But whatever has an infinite effect within its power at one and the same moment is infinite; therefore, etc.—The argument is also retouched in another way. At one and the same moment the first mover has in its power all the possible effects to be produced by motion. If the motion is endless, however, these effects are infinite, etc.

4.68 The consequence still does not seem to be validly established. Certainly not in the first way for a perfection does not increase simply because it endures for a greater length of time. Whiteness which exists for a year does not become any more perfect than if it existed for a day. Therefore, movement which continues for howsoever long a time, is not a more perfect effect than the movement which lasts for a day. Consequently, just because the agent has the effect in his power at one and the same moment we cannot infer there is a greater perfection involved in this case than in the other, except that here the agent moves by itself and for a longer time. And so we would have to prove that the eternity of the agent implied its infinity; otherwise, the latter could not be inferred merely from the endlessness of the movement.—What erases the second retouching is that we cannot infer any greater intensity in the perfection merely because the agent, as long as it exists, can produce successively any number whatsoever of the same species. For what an agent can do in one moment to one thing, by the very same power it can do to a thousand in a thousand such moments, if it exists for so long a time. However, according to the philosophers, who assumed only a finite number of species, the only infinity possible is the numerical infinity of effects that come to be and cease to be through change. Suppose someone else should prove that an infinity of species is possible by showing that some heavenly movements are incommensurable and so the same arrangement would never recur even though the movement should continue ad infinitum. In such a case, the infinite variety of [planetary] conjunctions would cause an infinite variety in the effects that can be produced. Whatever could be said of this view in itself, it is not the position of Aristotle, who would deny an infinity of species.

4.69 At this point, moreover, certain objections arise: [1] Why, in the first argument, do you try to prove infinity from the divine essence's knowledge of an infinity of things and here deny infinity can be inferred from its causing such, as if more were needed to make something exist in the mind than in reality? [2] Or how come you want to prove infinity in the second argument solely because the first being's nature is the total reason why it sees other things, yet you fail to prove it here from the fact that it is the total reason why another exists, for it is such at least as regards the nature just below it?

4.70 To the first objection: Wherever something can do many things at once, each requiring a peculiar perfection, from a greater number of such a more perfect thing can be inferred. Now this is the case with understanding an infinity of things at once. If you would prove the point, therefore, I would concede infinite power to whatever could produce simultaneously an infinity of things, but not if it can do so only successively.—But, you counter, this does possess such power at one and the same time. What is more, so far as itself is concerned, it could produce an infinity at once. It is only the nature of the effect that prevents this. What can cause both black and white is no less perfect because they cannot be produced simultaneously, for this comes from their mutual exclusiveness and not from any defect in the agent. My reply to this is: You have not proved that the first being is the total cause of this infinity or that it has the totality of this power at once, since what remains to be shown about its efficiency is that the second cause is not needed because of any causal power peculiar to the latter (though it has not been established that the formal possession of such power does not add something to the eminent possession of the same) . At one and the same time, therefore, the first being possesses eminently full causal power over every possible effect, even an infinity of such though these occur successively. I reply: This, so far as I see. is the final stroke needed to touch up the aforesaid consequence of Aristotle's argument. And from this I prove infinity as follows: If the first being at one and the same time formally possessed all causal power, even though the things which it could cause could not be given simultaneous existence, it would be infinite because—as far as it is concerned—it has power enough to produce an infinite number all at once, and the more one can produce simultaneously, the greater the power in intensity. But if the first being possessed such power in an even more perfect way than if it had it formally, its intensive infinity follows a fortiori. But the full causal power that each thing may have in itself the first being possesses even more perfectly than if it were formally present. Therefore, its power is infinite in intensity.

4.71 Even though I have put off treating omnipotence proper, as Catholics understand the term, to the Treatise on Things Believed, without proving omnipotence, we have proof of an infinite power which of itself has at once and in a more excellent way the fullness of causality, and on its part could produce at one time an infinity of things, if only they were able to exist simultaneously. If you object that the first cause on its part cannot produce at one time an infinity of effects, so long as it is not proved to be the total cause of these effects, this does not matter, since the requirements to be a total cause would not make it any more perfect than it would have to be if it were the first cause. This is clear, first of all, because secondary causes are not needed simply to supply some additional perfection to the causality, for if that were the case, the more remote effect would be the more perfect inasmuch as it would require a more perfect cause. But if secondary causes are needed in addition to the first cause, the reason according to the philosophers, lies in the fact that the effect is imperfect. That is to say, the first cause which immediately would be unable to cause anything imperfect, could do so in conjunction with another imperfect cause. Also, the first being, according to Aristotle, contains all the perfections in a more perfect manner than if they were formally present, were this latter possible. So it seems Aristotle's argument about an infinite power can be made to hold.

4.72 To the second objection above [4.69] I say that since the divine essence alone is the reason for seeing the stone perfectly, it follows that the stone adds nothing of perfection to that essence. But this does not follow if it is the reason for producing the stone immediately, even as total cause, for the first cause is the complete cause of the highest nature. But since the latter is finite, you cannot infer that its first cause is infinite; neither is it proved that the first is the total cause of other things.

4.73 [h. Some Ineffective Ways] Some, using this way of efficiency, infer [infinity] from the fact that [God] creates; [for] between the extremes of creation [viz. between nothing and something] there is an infinite gap. A word about the argument: If we take the antecedent to mean that a kind of durational period of non−existence preceded existence, then the fact that God creates is a postulate of faith; but if we understand this "precedence" of non−existence to be a kind of priority of nature as Avicenna does, then the antecedent is established from the nineteenth conclusion of the third chapter. For at least the first nature next to God does not exist of itself but is dependent upon him; neither is anything [viz. matter] presupposed for it to receive existence. Now "to be produced," as we have said, does not entail "to be changed," and if we take non−existence to be prior to existence by nature only, in this case there would be no extremes of change caused by this power. But whatever be said about the antecedent, the consequence remains unproved, for when there is no gap between the extremes, but they are said to be "distant" from one another in virtue of the extremes themselves, then the "distance" is as great as the greater extreme. Because God is infinite, for example, he is infinitely "distant" from a creature.

4.74 Finally some argue to the proposed conclusion from the absence of any intrinsic cause. Since form is limited by matter, any form incapable of being in matter therefore is infinite. I do not think this argument is any good, because [its proponents] admit an angel is immaterial, but not infinite. And existence will never limit [its] essence, since they hold that it is posterior to essence. Now the intrinsic degree of perfection that any entity has is not just a vicarious possession. Furthermore, it is a fallacy of the consequent to argue that just because form is limited with reference to matter, therefore without such reference it is unlimited. [This is like arguing] one body is limited with reference to another, hence where there is no such reference a body will be infinite; hence the outermost heaven will be infinite. This is the fallacy of the Physics, Bk. III. Just as a body is first limited in itself, so too with form. Form is first limited in itself (because there is just this sort of nature among things) before it is limited by matter since the latter limitation presupposes but does not cause the first. An essence is first finite by nature, and hence is unable to be made finite by existence; hence it is not subsequently limited by existence.

4.75 (Tenth Conclusion) From infinity every type of simplicity is inferred.

4.76 (1) Intrinsic simplicity in essence. If the essence were composed its components would be in themselves either finite or infinite. In the first case, the composite would be finite, in the second a part would not be less than the whole.

4.77 (2) It is not composed of quantitative parts, for infinite perfection is not characteristic of any magnitude [or quantity], for there can be no such thing as an infinite magnitude, and if the magnitude is finite, the greater would be the perfection. This is Aristotle's argument in the Physics, Bk. VIII, and the Metaphysics, Bk. XII.

4.78 Some one may object that a perfection infinite in magnitude would have the same formal character in the whole as in the part, hence there would be no greater perfection in a greater magnitude. The situation would be like that of the intellective soul, the most perfect form, which is as perfect in a small body as in a large one or as perfect in a part of the body as in the whole. Suppose that in essence it were of infinite power, that is, suppose it could know an infinity of intelligibles. It would so possess this power in a small magnitude that if the magnitude were increased, the power would become no greater. Hence the assumption that every power in a magnitude is greater the greater the magnitude is simply denied.—[By the way of an answer] Aristotle's argument can be retouched where he proves that an infinite perfection or power does not reside in magnitude in such a way that it is accidentally extended, viz. so that it is only partially in a part [of the magnitude], for then the power would be greater in the whole than in the part, not perhaps as regards its intensity but as far as the efficacy of its operation goes, like the case of a large fire and a part thereof. And thus it would follow that in a finite magnitude the power is not infinite in its efficacy. But if the power is extended in its efficacy, then it is not in itself of infinite intensity. Since we only infer a power to be infinite in itself from its infinite efficacy, this second consequence is clear. But for the first we have two proofs to show it follows: (I) In every aliquot part of a finite magnitude, power is only finite in efficacy; otherwise a part would not be less than the whole; hence in the whole also there is only a finite power, since every finite multiple of what is itself finite turns out to be a finite whole. (2) If you think of the magnitude as increasing, the efficacy of the power will be increased to that extent. But no matter how much you think of it as increasing, if it was finite to begin with, it will continue to remain so. So long as the power resides in a finite magnitude, however, you can always think of it as increasing. Hence it is only where the magnitude is infinite that this is no longer possible, so that in anything short of this no power is infinite in efficacy; neither then is any infinite in intensity. But what relevance to our thesis is the conclusion that a power infinite in intensity is not extended accidentally, so that it would be only partially in a part of the magnitude? How does this entail that the power is in magnitude in no way whatsoever? The final touch needed to complete the argument may be put in this way. What extension extends is a subject. This is not the infinite perfection itself or some matter of which it is the form, as the intellective [soul] is of the body, since this perfection does not exist in matter (from the first conclusion of this chapter). That is why the Philosopher prefaces his argument with proof that [such a power] is not in matter (Metaphysics, Bk. XII) . This last conclusion together with the previous one suffices to prove our thesis.

4.79 A shorter proof of the latter is this: To understand is not a subject of extension; the first nature is understanding (from the sixth conclusion of this chapter), and is not received in matter, so that one could speak of its quantity (from the first conclusion of this chapter).

4.80 (3) The infinite is not perfectible by any accidental addition. The reasons are these: [a] Everything perfectible lacks in itself the entity of the perfection; otherwise it would not be of such perfection only potentially. The perfection, therefore, is added to the perfectible and the combination is more perfect than either of the components. The infinite lacks nothing; neither does anything able to be united with it add anything to its perfection; otherwise something could be greater than the infinite.—[b] Secondly, since it lacks quantity or dimensions, material accidents cannot exist in it. Neither does it have any immaterial accidents pertaining to the intellect or the will, since such things as understanding and volition which would seem most likely to be accidents are identified with its [substance] (from the sixth conclusion of this chapter).

4.81 Another proof advanced for this is that nothing is incidental [per accidens] to the first being, because: [c] what is essential [per se] is prior to everything incidental; [d] in the first being nothing is caused and [e] nothing is potential. Now while this argument shows that an accident is not of the essence of the first being, it does not prove that such a thing is not there incidentally. The first reason [c] does not, for while there would be nothing merely incidental in the first being's essence, which was there first, there could be something else produced by this essence which just happens to be there; and hence there is indeed something essential which is prior to this incidental thing, since the first essence would be prior to the union of the accident with it. The second reason [d] does not prove the point, because the first essence would be uncaused, even if something caused happened to modify it. Of every substance that is produced, it is true that the essence is not its own cause, but in some cases the essence is the cause of its accidents. The third reason [e] is no proof, because potentiality to what is incidental is only potentiality in a qualified sense. But how do you show such potentiality cannot exist in something which is actual only as to its essence?

4.82 [f] Another reason given is that in the first being there is nothing but pure perfection (from the second conclusion of this chapter); every such perfection however is identical with its essence; otherwise it would not be the best of itself, or else more than one thing would be the best in an unqualified sense.—This argument too is not conclusive, for from what was said about the sixth proof for the fourth conclusion of this chapter [4.22], it is clear that there is nothing inconsistent with the notion of pure perfection that there be many such traits each of which is the highest of its own kind and nevertheless one highest thing is better than another, and the essence of the first thing is better than all these highest things whether taken singly or all together, even though none of these traits are the same as its essence, but only inherent in it. For this does not follow: There is a characteristic trait which is better than any other mutually exclusive trait, and it is found in something which, so far as this trait is concerned, is supreme– therefore this thing is supreme in an unqualified sense. All that follows is: Therefore, this thing is the best of the entire class of things which either have this trait or have some trait which mutually excludes this trait. If all the perfections that are called pure would include each other by way of identity, whatever would have one in a more perfect way would also have the others in a more perfect way. Now such is not the case: matter is more necessary than form, but it is less actual; an accident depends upon a substance, yet it may be simpler than the substance. Similarly, the heavens are less perishable than a composite substance, yet our animated body, qua animated, is a more noble thing. Hence it follows that pure perfections, except for some that are attributes of being, differ from one another and perhaps from their subject; and one can be had in a high degree whereas the other may not be there to that same degree or may not be there at all.—What is more, the first proposition of this argument has not been established [viz. in the first being there is nothing but pure perfection], for the second [conclusion of this chapter], which is cited as proof, applies only to what is intrinsic to the highest nature and not to what is there by way of accident. If some contentious individual were to assume that in the first being there is something accidental, it would be difficult to prove against him that the latter is a pure perfection, for at times a more noble nature is characterized by a less noble trait and a less noble nature by a more noble trait that happens to be a pure perfection. Prime matter, for example, is simple whereas man is not; simplicity is such a trait [i.e. a pure perfection].

4.83 Indeed, it would be difficult, if not impossible, to prove by the last four reasons [viz. c–f] that the first being has no accident inherent only contingently and incidentally in virtue of which it can be accidentally changed either by itself or by something posterior to it. For even though we postulate a first cause in regard to our actions, we assume that our will produces the change in itself that we call willing. If it could be solidly proved that an accident would be repugnant to the simplicity of the first nature, this would indeed be a fruitful conclusion. If anyone is not satisfied with the first two proofs given here [4.80] let him bring forth better ones.

4.84 O Lord, our God, Catholics can infer most of the perfections which philosophers knew of you from what has been said. You are the first efficient cause, the ultimate end, supreme in perfection, transcending all things. You are uncaused in any way and therefore incapable of becoming or perishing; indeed it is simply impossible that you should not exist for of yourself you are necessary being. You are therefore eternal, because the span of your existence is without limit and you experience it all at once for it cannot be strung out in a succession of events. For there can be no succession save in what is being continually caused or at least in what is dependent for its existence upon another, and this dependence is a far cry from what has necessary being of itself. You live a most noble life, because you are understanding and volition. You are happy, indeed you are by nature happiness, because you are in possession of yourself. You are the clear vision of yourself and the most joyful love, and although you are most self–sufficient and happy in yourself alone, you still understand in a single act everything that can be known. At one and the same time you possess the power to freely and contingently will each thing that can be caused and by willing it through your volition to cause it to be. Most truly then you are of infinite power. You are incomprehensible, infinite, for nothing omniscient or of infinite power is finite, nor supreme among beings. Neither is the ultimate end, nor what exists of itself in all simplicity, something finite. You are the ultimate in simplicity, having no really distinct parts, or no realities in your essence which are not really the same. In you no quantity, no accident can be found. and therefore you are incapable of accidental change, even as I have already expressed, you are in essence immutable. You alone are simply perfect, not just a perfect angel, or a perfect body, but a perfect being, lacking no entity it is possible for anything to have. Nothing can formally possess every entity but every entity can exist in something either formally or eminently, as it does in you, O God, who are supreme among beings, the only one of them who is infinite. Communicating the rays of your goodness most liberally, you are boundless good, to whom as the most lovable thing of all every single being in its own way comes back to you as to its ultimate end.

4.85 You alone are the first truth. Indeed, the false is not what it seems to be. Hence something besides itself is the basis for what it appears to be, for were its nature alone the basis, it would appear to be what it really is. But for you there is no other ground or basis for what appears, because in your essence which is first apparent to yourself all things appear, and by that very fact nothing subsequent is the basis for what appears to you. In that essence, I say, whatever can be known in all the fullness of its meaning is present to your intellect. You are then truth in all its splendor, infallible truth, comprehending every intelligible truth with certainty. For the other things apparent to you do not seem to exist in you in such a way that they deceive you simply because they appear in you. For the ground or reason for the appearance does not prevent the proper meaning of what it reveals from appearing to your intellect as is the case with our visual deceptions, when the appearance of something else prevents us from seeing what is really there. This is not so in your intellect; quite the contrary, so perfect in its clarity is the vision of your essence that whatever is displayed therein appears to you in all its proper meaning. For my purposes there is no need to treat at greater length the subject of your truth or of the ideas in you. Much indeed has been said about the ideas, but even were it never said, indeed, were the ideas never mentioned, no less will be known of your perfection. This is clear, because your essence is the perfect ground for knowing each and every thing that can be known to the extent that it can be known. He who wishes may call this an idea, but here I do not care to dwell further upon this Greek and Platonic word.

4.86 Besides the aforesaid points which the philosophers have affirmed of you, Catholics often praise you as omnipotent, immense, omnipresent, just yet merciful, provident of all creatures but looking after intellectual ones in a special way, but these matters are deferred to the next tract. In this first treatise I have tried to show how the metaphysical attributes affirmed of you can be inferred in some way by natural reason. In the tract which follows, those shall be set forth that are the subject of belief, wherein reason is held captive—yet to Catholics, the latter are the more certain since they rest firmly upon your own most solid truth and not upon our intellect which is blind and weak in many things.

4.87 But there is one thing more that I include here which I do not think that reason is unable to prove, and which will provide the finishing touch to this little work, namely (Eleventh conclusion) You are one God, than whom there is no other as you have declared through the Prophet.

4.88 In support of this conclusion. I propose five propositions any one of which if proved, entails the initial thesis:(1) Numerically there is but one infinite intellect; (2) Numerically there is but one infinite will; (3) Numerically there is but one infinite power; (4) Numerically there is but one necessary being; (5) There is but one infinite goodness. That the proposed conclusion follows from each is clear enough. They are proved in order.

4.89 First of all the first: An infinite intellect knows everything most perfectly, i.e. to the extent that it is intelligible; and in knowing such a thing it is not dependent upon anything else, for otherwise it would not be infinite. If two such intellects existed (call them A and B), both would lack perfect independent intellection. For A, if it knows B through B, depends upon B for its knowledge of B, as an act depends upon an object when the two are not the same. If A, on the contrary, knows B not through B but through itself, it will not know B as perfectly as B is intelligible, because nothing is perfectly present unless it be there in itself, or in something which contains it in a most excellent way: A itself does not contain B. If you should say that it is like B, I would counter: Knowledge through what is similar is merely knowledge under a universal aspect, to the extent that the things are alike. Through such a universal what properly distinguishes each would remain unknown. Furthermore, such a knowledge through a universal is not intuitive but abstractive, and intuitive knowledge is the more perfect of the two. Also, one and the same act does not have two adequate objects. A is its own adequate object, and therefore it does not know B.

4.90 Secondly, we prove the proposition about the infinite will. Such a will supremely loves what is supremely lovable; but A does not love B supremely, both (a) because, if by nature it loves itself more, then also by a free and upright will it loves itself more; and (b) because it would be made happy by B; and yet if B were destroyed, it would be no less happy. It is impossible then that one and the same thing should be beatified by two, yet this would follow were there two such wills; for A does not use B, therefore it rests in B as its end; therefore A is happy in B.

4.91 The third proposition about infinite power is proved thus: If there were two infinite powers each would be first with reference to the same set of things because essential dependence is referred to the nature and equally to everything in the nature. The same things cannot depend on two first [causes] (from the sixteenth conclusion of the third chapter); more than one first ruler, therefore, is not good, for either it is impossible, or else the rule of each will be restricted and each only partially in control. And the further question arises, in virtue of what single bond are they joined in ruling.

4.92 The fourth proposition about a necessary being is proved thus: If a species is capable of existing in more than one individual, then so far as the species itself is concerned, it is capable of existing in an infinity of such; therefore if a necessary being can be multiplied, there can be an infinity of necessary things; consequently they also exist; for whatever is necessary cannot exist if it does not exist.

4.93 The fifth about the good is shown in this way: Many good things are better than one when each adds goodness to the other; but nothing is better than an infinite good. The argument here is as follows: any will is set at rest completely by the one infinite good; but if there were another, one could rightly wish that both exist rather than one alone; therefore the will would not be fully satisfied with the single infinite good.—Other means of proof could be adduced, but for now let these suffice.

4.94 O Lord our God! You are one in nature. You are one in number. Truly have you said that besides you there is no God. For though many may be called gods or thought to be gods, you alone are by nature God. You are the true God from whom, in whom and through whom all things are; you are blessed forever. Amen!

Here ends the tract of John [Duns] Scotus about the first principle.

Appendix

Two Questions From Lectures On Bk. I Of The Sentences

[Question One: Does an infinite being exist?]

The first question raised in connection with the second distinction is this: "In the realm of beings is there some being which is actually infinite?"

[Pro et Contra]

It would seem not, for:

[Arg. I] If one of two contraries were actually infinite, it would be incompatible with anything other than itself. But good and evil are contraries. Hence, if some good were actually infinite, nothing would be actually evil, which is false.

2 In answer to this some say that the evil in the universe is not a true contrary to God or the infinite good, because he has no true contrary. But this is no solution, for whether the contrariety be formal or only virtual between two things, if one of the two be infinite, it will tolerate nothing contrary either to itself or to its effect. If the sun, for instance, possessed infinite heat either formally or virtually, nothing would be cold. Consequently, if some good were actually infinite either virtually or formally, then throughout the universe evil, as the contrary of some good, would be simply non−existent.

3 [Arg. II] An infinite body would not allow another body to coexist; therefore an infinite

spirit will not allow another spirit to coexist. The antecedent is evident from Bk. IV of the Physics. The consequence is thus proved: just as two bodies cannot coexist in one place because of their opposed dimensions, so neither does it seem possible for two spirits because their actualizations are opposed.

4 Another proof of the same consequence is this: if another body could coexist with an infinite body, then there would be something larger than an infinite body. It would seem then that if another spirit existed in addition to the infinite, there would be something virtually greater than the infinite.

5 [Arg. III] Furthermore, whatever is here and nowhere else is limited in its whereabouts; what exists now but not then is of limited time; and what acts by this action and no other is limited in action, and so on. But whatever exists is a "this" in such a way that it is no other; therefore it is finite, whatever it be.

6 [Arg. IV] Furthermore, if some power were infinite, it would cause movement instantaneously, as Bk. VIII of the Physics proves. Motion, therefore, would occur instantaneously, which is impossible.

7 To the contrary:

In Bk. VIII of the Physics, the Philosopher says that the first mover is infinite. And therefore his power does not reside in any magnitude—not in an infinite magnitude, because there is no such thing, nor in a finite magnitude, because something of greater magnitude would have a greater power. But this argument is not valid unless it be understood of something that is infinite in power, because a body, like the sun, would be infinite in duration.

[Question Two: Is it self–evident that an infinite being exists?]

8 This poses the further question: Is the existence of something infinite, such as God's existence, a fact that is self–evident?

[Pro et Contra]

A TREATISE ON GOD AS FIRST PRINCIPLE

The arguments that it is are these:

[Arg. I] Damascene says in the first chapter: "The knowledge that God exists is implanted in everyone." Such knowledge, however, is self-evident, as is clear from Bk. II of the Metaphysics, where first principles, which are like the [proverbial] door, are presented as something self-evident.

9 [Arg. II] Furthermore, the existence of a thing is self-evident if it is impossible to think of anything greater than it. For if one were to grant the opposite of the predicate, it would destroy the subject; because if the thing in question did not exist one could think of something greater, viz. its existence, which is greater than its non-existence. And this seems to be Anselm's argument in chapter two of the Proslogion.

10 [Arg. III] That truth exists is self-evident; therefore etc. Proof of the antecedent: Whatever follows from its own denial is self-evident. But truth is such, because if you affirm that truth exists, then it is true that you affirm this and hence truth exists; if you may deny that truth exists, then it would –be true that truth does not exist. And therefore some truth still exists.

11 [Arg. IV] Furthermore, those propositions are self-evident which derive their necessity from that fact that their terms have at least that qualified existence that comes from being in the mind. All the more then is that proposition self-evident which owes its necessity to the being of the thing and terms in an unqualified sense. But "God exists" is such a proposition. Proof of the antecedent: Suppose that neither a whole nor its part existed. The very fact that these terms in the mind are related the way they are, guarantees "Every whole is greater than its part" to be a necessary truth. In such a case, however, the terms would have only a qualified existence in the mind.

12 To the contrary:

No mind can deny what is self-evident: but God's existence can be denied for "The fool says in his heart, 'There is no God'" [Psalms 13,1].

[I. Reply to the Second Question]

13 We must answer this second question first. To solve it, we must understand first of all what is meant by a self—evident proposition. Then it will be clear if "God exists" (or some other proposition in which "existence" is predicated of something belonging to God, such as "An infinite being exists") is self—evident.

14 To understand the meaning of "self—evident proposition," know that when a proposition is said to be such, the word 'self' does not rule out every cause whatsoever, because it does not exclude knowledge of the terms. For no proposition is self—evident unless there is knowledge of its terms. What is excluded is any cause or reason which is not essentially included in the concepts of the terms of the self—evident proposition. Hence, that proposition is self—evident which does not need to borrow knowledge elsewhere, but draws the evidence of its own truth from the knowledge of its terms and has the sole source of its certitude within itself.

15 But the name, now, is one term and the concept associated with it is another, the difference between them being that of a name and its definition. Proof: In a demonstration, the definition of one of the extremes serves as a middle term, the remaining term in the premises being the same as in the conclusion. The extreme differs from the middle term as the defined differs from the definition. If the term and concept of the thing defined were the same as that of the definition, then the most cogent form of demonstration would involve a begging of the question. What is more, it would have but two terms. Consequently, the concept of the definition is different from that of the thing defined in so far as the latter is expressed by the name which is defined.

16 Furthermore, Bk. I of the Physics says that much the same thing happens in the relation of names to their definitions as does in the relation of the whole to its parts. The thing defined is known even before its definition is discovered by an analysis of the parts it has. Wherefore, in so far as the concept of the definition is expressed by the name of the thing defined, it is something confused and is known before [the definition]. But it is expressed more distinctly by the name of the definition, which distinguishes the several parts of the defined. Hence the concept associated with the name of the thing defined is other than that of the definition.

17 From this it follows that a proposition is not self—evident if our only knowledge of it stems from a definition of its terms. For, inasmuch as only that proposition is self—evident which is evident from a knowledge of its terms, and the definition and the

name are different terms, it follows that a proposition whose evidence stems exclusively from the definition of its terms, is not self–evident, since it borrows its evidence from something beyond itself and it can be a conclusion with reference to some other proposition.

18 Likewise, if a proposition whose evidence stemmed from the definition of its terms were self–evident, then every proposition would be self–evident that is in the first mode of per se predication, such as "Man is an animal, and a body" and so on, up to "substance." Consequently, knowledge of the definition is not enough to make a proposition self–evident.

19 Therefore that proposition only is self–evident which draws its evidence solely from the knowledge of its terms and does not borrow it from the evidence for other concepts.

20 From this we see there is no point or purpose in distinguishing propositions which are self–evident by their nature from those which are self–evident to us; or among the latter, those which are self–evident to the wise from those which are self–evident to the foolish; or those which are self–evident of the first order from those which are self–evident of the second order. For a proposition is not called self–evident because it happens to be in a particular mind, but because its terms are by their nature apt to cause self–evident knowledge in any intellect which conceives them as self–evident in themselves. And therefore nothing is self–evident which can be demonstrated to any intellect. Nevertheless, grades do exist among self–evident propositions according to their value or lack of it. Thus, "It is impossible for the same thing to both be and not be" is of more value than this: "Every whole is greater than its part," etc.

21 Secondly, turning now to the question at issue, I say this: Suppose one means by the name "God" something which we do not conceive perfectly—such as "this divine essence" where the latter term is grasped as self–evident, as would be the case, for instance, if God, seeing himself, were to impose this name "God" upon his essence. Then one might ask whether "God exists" or "This essence exists" would be self–evident. I say that they would be, because the terms in this case are such that they are able to make such a proposition evident to anyone who grasped the terms of the proposition perfectly, and "self–evident" could not be more aptly applied than to this essence.

22 But suppose you ask whether existence is predicated of any concept which we have of God's essence, so that such a proposition would be self–evident wherein existence is predicated of such a concept, as when we say for example that "The infinite exists." To this I say: No! For nothing which can be the conclusion of a demonstration is self–evident from the knowledge of its terms. But every proposition predicating existence of any concept we have of God is just such, viz. the conclusion of a demonstration. Proof: Anything which pertains to a more comprehensive but less extensive concept according to the first mode of per se predication, can also be shown to pertain per se to a broader concept by using the more comprehensive concept as a middle term. For instance, if some attribute pertains primarily to "triangle," it can be demonstrated to be an attribute of "figure" by means of "triangle." Every concept that we use to conceive of God, however, is less comprehensive than "this essence." Therefore, by using as middle term "this essence" to which existence primarily pertains, one could demonstrate existence of every concept that we use to conceive of God. Consequently, no proposition such as "An infinite being exists" is self–evident from a knowledge of its terms but it borrows its evidence from something else, and hence is not self–evident.—The major of this argument, however, can be asserted in an even more universal form, viz. whatever pertains to something primarily, does not pertain to another except in virtue of that nature to which it belongs primarily. But "existence" belongs primarily to "this divine nature." Therefore it is not ascribed [primarily] to some property [of this essence], neither does it pertain to any other [divine attribute] except in virtue of the nature of [the divine] essence. Therefore, no proposition in which existence is predicated of some property of this [divine] essence which we conceive is primarily true, but it is true only by reason of some other truth, and consequently it is not a primary or self–evident proposition.

23 Furthermore, if a proposition is self–evident, then any intellect which conceives its terms, will by that very fact know that the proposition is true. But this is not the case with such a proposition as "God exists"—where by God is meant not this essence which we conceive, but some concept which we have about this essence—or "God is infinite" or "An infinite being exists." Therefore, it is not self–evident. The major is evident. The minor is established as follows. Every one who assents to any proposition either because of faith or belief or because it is demonstrated, grasps the meaning of the terms. But we assent to this: "God exists" either because of faith or because of a demonstration. Therefore, the meaning of the terms are known prior to faith or demonstration. But this apprehending of the terms does not make us assent to the proposition, otherwise we should not know it only by faith or demonstration.

24 What is more, there is a third argument. To understand it, you must keep in mind first of all that some concepts are simply simple and others are not. That concept is simply simple which is not reduced to some prior or simpler concept, nor is it fully resolved into more than one concept. Such are the concepts of being, and of the ultimate differences. But a concept that is not simply simple is one which, though it be simply grasped, i.e. nothing is affirmed or denied about it, is nevertheless resolved into more than one concept of which the one can be conceived without the other. Such is the concept of the species which can be resolved into a genus and a difference. Consequently, even though a concept be simple in the sense that nothing is affirmed or denied, one must distinguish further whether it is simply simple or not in the aforesaid sense. From this it is clear how one should understand or explain the statement of the Philosopher in Bk. IX of the Metaphysics where we read that so far as simple concepts are concerned the deception characteristic of what is composite is absent. It is not a question here of an affirmation or negation of anything, for one can err by asserting something of a simple concept just as one can say something true or false of a composite concept. What he has in mind is that "the definition of the composite is a long rigmarole," in which many concepts are lumped together and error can arise concerning their conjunction. Sometimes the combination may even include contradictory elements as is the case with "dead man" [i.e. a man without a soul] or "irrational man" [where man is defined as a rational animal]. But such is not the case where simple notions are concerned, for here either one grasps the whole or he grasps nothing.

25 Keeping this explanation in mind, I argue as follows: No proposition about a concept which is not simply simple will be self-evident, unless it also be self-evident that the components of such a concept go together, as I shall prove. Every proper concept that we have of God, however, is not simply simple and consequently, nothing is self-evident of such a concept unless we know that the parts of such a concept essentially go together. But, as I shall prove shortly, it is not self-evident that this is the case. As a consequence, no proposition in which any thing is asserted of any concept we have of God will be self-evident, e.g. "God exists" or "An infinite God exists."

26 Proof of the major: no notion is true of anything unless it first be true in itself. For if it is false in itself, it will not be true of anything. This is clear from Bk. V of the Metaphysics in the chapter "About the False," where the Philosopher intends to say that the false in itself includes a contradiction, whereas what is false of something is that which is not false of everything whatsoever, as is the case with the false in itself.

Consequently, it is necessary that one must first know that a thing is true in itself before one can know that it is true of something. But if one does not grasp that the parts of a concept that is not simply simple go together, he does not conceive something that is true in itself and hence does not conceive it as being in something or as true of something. Nothing therefore is self–evidently known about a concept which is not simply simple unless one first recognizes that the parts of this concept go together.

27 The other proposition assumed in the argument is also true, viz. that every concept which we have of God is not simply simple, because every such concept I have of God has to do with what is common to me and to him, as will become clear later.

28 The other assumption is true too, viz. that it is not self–evident that the parts of the concept we use to think of God go together, because it can be demonstrated that one part goes with the other, as is the case, for example, when we demonstrate "God is infinite" or "God exists" (where by "God" we mean what we conceive God to be).

29 From this it is clear that they are incorrect who claim such propositions as "God exists," "A necessary being exists," or "What is operating is in act" are self–evidently known on the grounds that the opposite of the predicate is inconsistent with the subject, and therefore the proposition is self–evident. I say that they are not self–evident, because whenever you use a concept that is not simply simple as the subject you must have self–evident knowledge that the parts go together, which is not the case with "A necessary being exists" and "What is operating is in act", for it is not self–evident that something necessary exists, but this can be demonstrated. That is why the Heracliteans were wont to deny "necessary being" and assert that all is in continuous motion. It is the same with "What is operating is in act," because it is not self–evident that there is actually anything which is operating. Hence it does not follow from the fact that the opposite of the predicate is inconsistent with the subject that the proposition in question is necessary. Indeed, it may even be that such a proposition is false, as is the case with "An irrational man is an animal": for this is inconsistent: "No animal exists, yet an irrational man exists." It is the same with the proposition: "Something greater than God exists," which is false, even though the opposite of the predicate is inconsistent with the subject.

30 If you insist that the predicate is already posited in the subject in the proposition like "A necessary being exists" or "What is operating is in act" and consequently they are self–evident, I reply that this does not follow, because it is not self–evidently known that

the notions which are presumed to be present in the subject can actually go together.

31 To this it is objected on logical grounds that if the opposite of the predicate of some proposition is inconsistent with the subject, then from the existence of the subject follows the existence of the predicate. For example, in the proposition "Man is an animal," the opposite of animal is inconsistent with man; therefore this follows: "If a man exists, an animal exists." Hence, if in the proposition "An irrational man is an animal," the opposite of the predicate is inconsistent with the subject, then this would follow: "An irrational man exists, therefore an animal exists." Hence the medium used to infer this, viz. "An irrational man is an animal," is true. Therefore, if the opposite of the predicate is inconsistent with the subject, the proposition will be true and necessary. To this I say: the inference does not follow, because those extremes must be united for which the inference holds. But in this." An irrational man exists, therefore an animal exists," the consequence holds solely because of "man" and not because of "irrational," and therefore it is by virtue of "Man is an animal" that it holds. Consequently, the following is not an inference: "An irrational man exists, therefore a man exists," because "irrational" adds nothing to the inference, and to go from one thing to the same thing is not an inference; neither then is this: "A necessary being exists, therefore it exists."

32 And so it is clear, then, first of all what a self–evident proposition is, seeing that it is one which draws its evidence from the concepts of its terms and from nothing else, whatever be the intellect which conceives those terms. For this follows what was said above [Cf. 14–20]

33 It is also clear in what way "God exists" is self–evident and in what way it is not. For if we mean by God "this divine essence" which we do not conceive, it is a self–evident truth; but if we mean by God, that which we first conceive God to be in such universal terms as "first principle" and "infinite" and many such like, then the truth is not self–evidently known, as has already been shown.

[II. To the Arguments at the Beginning of the Second Question (par. 8–11)]

34 [To Arg. I] As for the first reason, based on Damascene's statement that the knowledge of God is implanted in all, I say that in the same place he says that "no one knows God except by revelation" so that it is necessary to gloss his statement. Therefore it can be said that the cognition of God is implanted in everybody, not in particular but in

universal terms and according to common notions which are most appropriately applied to God, and therefore by way of appropriation it is said that the knowledge of him is implanted in all. Hence "being" and "act", etc. are most appropriately applied to God. Or one could say that the knowledge of God is implanted in everyone by reason of their knowledge of creatures, from which they come to know God. But even for him the knowledge of God is not self−evident.

35 [To Arg. II] As for the other, where it is argued that according to Anselm the existence of a thing is self−evident, if it is impossible to think of anything greater, I reply that such is not the case. Hence Anselm's intention there is not to show that the existence of God is self−evident, but that it is true. And he makes two syllogisms, of which the first is: "Something is greater than anything which does not exist; but nothing is greater than the highest; therefore the highest is not non−being." There is another syllogism: "What is not a non−being, exists; but the highest is not a non−being, therefore the highest exists."

36 [To Arg. III] As for the other reason, where it is claimed: "That truth exists is self−evident", I say for one thing the argument fallaciously affirms the consequent, since it proceeds from truth in general to this "Truth" which is God. For another, I say that it is not self−evident that "truth exists." And when it is argued that "If truth does not exist, it is true that truth does not exist," I say that the consequence does not follow, because there is no truth except fundamentally in things and formally in the intellect. But if nothing is true, then nothing exists and consequently in nothing is there truth. Hence, it doesn't follow that if truth does not exist, therefore this dictum "Truth does not exist" is true.

37 [To Arg. IV] As for the next argument, when it is claimed that the proposition "God exists" has terms which are purely necessary, whereas this is not the case with "Every whole is greater than a part thereof" I say that the necessity of the proposition is not a necessity characteristic of real things, but it consists of the evidence for the proposition which is in the mind because the terms are there. "God exists," however, has a necessity and an evidence that stems from reality, but the other proposition has the greater evidence in the mind, once its terms are known, and consequently it is self−evident, whereas the other is not.

[III. Reply to the First Question]

38 In answer to the first question one must say this. Some properties of the infinite being have reference to creatures and from the existence of their referents, the existence of these properties can be inferred. From this it follows that the proper way to know the existence of God and his infinity is by way of such divine properties as have reference to creatures.

A. God's existence demonstrated from properties which refer to creatures

39 Now there are two properties of God which have reference to creatures, one is eminence in goodness, the other is causality. Eminence is not subdivided further, but causality is. According to some, its divisions are: exemplar, efficient and final cause. Such say that the exemplar cause gives a thing its essential being. But I say here (and later on in more detail) that the exemplar cause is not to be numbered alongside of the efficient cause, for it is only as a concomitant factor of an efficient cause that the exemplar in the mind of the artisan gives any being to a thing. And if [the exemplar in view of its effect] can be considered as a formal cause, then it would pertain to eminence rather than to causality, for the more excellent being contains virtually the forms of other things and contains them unitively. Hence in God there are these three: eminence, efficiency and finality.

1. The Argument from Efficiency

40 Now efficiency can be considered either as a metaphysical or as a physical property. The metaphysical property is more extensive than the physical for "to give existence to another" is of broader scope than "to give existence by way of movement or change." And even if all existence were given in the latter fashion, the notion of the one is still not that of the other.

It is not efficiency as a physical attribute, however, but efficiency as the metaphysician considers it that provides a more effective way of proving God's existence, for there are more attributes in metaphysics than in physics whereby the existence of God can be established. It can be shown, for example, from "composition and simplicity," from "act and potency," from "one and many," from those features which are properties of being. Wherefore, if you find one extreme of the disjunction imperfectly realized in a creature, you conclude that the alternate, the perfect extreme exists in God.

A TREATISE ON GOD AS FIRST PRINCIPLE

Averroes, therefore, in attacking Avicenna at the end of Bk. I of the Physics is incorrect when he claims that to prove that God exists is the job of the physicist alone, because this can be established only by way of motion, and in no other way—as if metaphysics began with a conclusion which was not evident in itself, but needed to be proved in physics (For Averroes asserts this falsehood at the end of the first book of the Physics). In point of fact, however, [God's existence] can be shown more truly and in a greater variety of ways by means of those metaphysical attributes which characterize being. The proof lies in this that the first efficient cause imparts not merely this fluid existence [called motion] but existence in an unqualified sense, which is still more perfect and widespread. Now the existence of a primacy in the higher class does not follow logically from the existence of a primary in a lower [or more specific] class, unless that member is the most noble. For example, this does not follow: "The most noble donkey exists, therefore the most noble animal exists." Consequently, from the property of being the most noble being, one can argue better to a primacy among beings than from the primacy characteristic of a prime mover.

41 Hence, we omit the physical argument by which a prime mover is shown to exist and, using the efficiency characteristic of beings, we argue that among beings there is one which is a first efficient cause. And this is Richard's argument in Bk. I, chapter eight On the Trinity.

Some being is not eternal, and therefore it does not exist of itself, neither is it caused by nothing, because nothing produces itself. Hence, it is from some other being. The latter either gives existence in virtue of something other than itself or not. And its existence, too, it either gets from another or not. If neither be true—i.e., if it neither imparts existence in virtue of another nor receives its own existence from another—then this is the first efficient cause, for such is the meaning of the term. But if either of the above alternatives holds [viz. if it receives existence, or imparts it to others only in virtue of another], then I inquire about the latter as I did before. One cannot go on this way ad infinitum. Hence, we end up with some first efficient cause, which neither imparts existence in virtue of another nor receives its own existence from another.

42 Objections, however, are raised against this argument. To begin with, it seems to beg the question, for it assumes that there is an order and a first among causes. But if no efficient cause is first, then both the order and the terminus in such causes would have to be denied.

43 Furthermore, inasmuch as the argument begins with a contingent premise, it does not seem to be a demonstration. For a demonstration proceeds from necessary premises, and everything exists contingently which owes its existence to God. Consequently, with reference to God this statement is contingent: "Some being is non–eternal," because from it this statement follows: "Some non–eternal being exists," and this latter is contingent.

44 Furthermore, since there is no demonstration of the reasoned fact, neither does there seem to be any demonstration of the simple fact. For, whenever some conclusion is established by a demonstration of the latter type, one can always set up a converse demonstration of the reasoned fact (from cause to effect). But from the existence of the first cause, the existence of other things cannot be inferred by a demonstration of the reasoned fact; therefore, neither is the converse relation demonstrable as a simple fact.

45 To solve these objections, then, know this to begin with. Incidental [per accidens] causes are not the same as causes that are ordered to one another incidentally, just as essential [per se] causes are not the same as causes essentially ordered to one another. For when I speak of essential [i.e. per se] and incidental [i.e. per accidens] causes, I express a one to one relationship, viz. between a cause and its effect. But when causes are said to be incidentally or essentially ordered, two causes are being considered with reference to a single effect, so that we have a two to one relationship. Now causes are essentially ordered if one is ordered to the other so that [together] they cause a third thing, the effect. But causes are incidentally ordered if one is not ordered to the other in the very act of causing the effect. This would be the case with father and grandfather with regard to the son.

46 Secondly, it follows from this that essentially ordered causes differ from incidentally ordered causes in a threefold way:

The first difference is this: one cause depends essentially upon the other in order to produce an effect, which is not the case with causes that are ordered to a single effect only incidentally. Wherefore, the single causality of one of the incidentally ordered causes suffices to produce the single effect, whereas the causality of only one of the essentially ordered causes does not suffice.

47 From this, the second difference follows, viz. where essentially ordered causes are concerned, their causality differs in kind and they are not related to their effect in the

same way. But the causality of all the incidentally ordered causes is of the same kind, since they can be referred immediately to the same effect.

48 From this, too, the third difference arises, viz. that the causalities of all of the essentially ordered causes concur simultaneously to produce the effect. For what is needed to cause an effect is that all its necessary causes concur. But all the essentially ordered causes are necessary causes. Therefore, all such must actually concur to bring about the effect. But this is not required where incidentally ordered causes are concerned, because each of itself possesses perfect causality as regards its effect, and they are of one kind so far as their immediate effect is concerned.

49 With these things presupposed, then, what remains to be shown is that the proof for a first cause does not involve a begging of the question. Therefore, I first prove that there is such a first where essentially ordered causes are concerned. I do this:

First, by the argument of the Philosopher, Bk. II of the Metaphysics (and that of Avicenna, too, Bk. VIII, chapter one) which seems to be this: All causes intermediate between the first and the last, cause by virtue of the first, so that their causality is derived from the first. As the Philosopher points out there, it is not derived from the last but from the first, for if "to cause" pertains to any of them, a fortiori it will pertain to the first. Now the minor of his argument seems to be this: "If the series of causes is infinite then all are intermediate causes." Consequently they all cause in virtue of some first cause, so that it is necessary to assume a first among efficient causes.

50 But you may object: When you say in the minor, "Every cause in an infinite series is an intermediate cause," either you mean by intermediate such causes as lie between a first and a last in the series, and so assume that there is a first, or else you mean it in a purely negative sense [i.e. as being neither the first nor last], in which case there are four terms, and again the conclusion does not follow.

51 I say, therefore, that the statement first assumed by the Philosopher is not the major in the argument, but is antecedent thereto. The argument, consequently, goes in this way. Every intermediary cause having a first and a last, derives its causality from the first. Hence the causality of the intermediary causes comes from the first. But if there were an infinity of such causes, they would all be intermediary. Hence, their causality is derived from some first. But if they are infinite, then there is no first. Hence, there is and there is

not a first cause!

Proof of the aforesaid consequence:

All causes in anyway intermediate, be they positively or negatively so, are caused. Therefore, the whole concatenation of intermediary causes is caused. Hence, it is caused by something which is outside the concatenated series. Hence, there is a first.

52 What is more, the causalities of all the essential causes must concur simultaneously to produce their effect, as was pointed out above. But an infinity of things cannot so concur to produce one thing, hence there is not an infinity of such causes and therefore a first cause does exist.

53 Furthermore, a cause which is prior as regards the causation has a more perfect causality, and the more it is prior, the more perfect its causality. Hence, a cause with infinite priority would have an infinite causality. But if there were an infinite regress in essentially ordered causes, then there is a cause with infinite priority. To assume an infinite regress, then, is to grant a cause whose causality is infinite. But surely a cause which exercises infinite causality when it causes, does not depend upon anything else, and as such it would be the first. Therefore, etc.

54 Furthermore, to be able to produce something is not a property which of itself entails imperfection. But whatever is of such like is able to exist in something without imperfection. And thus there must be an efficient cause in which it can exist in this way, which is impossible if the cause does not produce its effect independently, and this means it is the first efficient cause. Therefore, etc.

55 Likewise, if one assumes an infinity of incidentally ordered causes, it still follows that there is a first in essentially ordered causes, for those causes which are incidentally ordered are in individuals of the same species. Then [one argues] as follows: No deformity is perpetual, unless it is brought about by a perpetual cause—outside this coordination—which perpetuates this deformity. Proof: Nothing that is part of this concatenation can be the cause of the whole of this perpetuated deformity, because in such incidentally ordered [causes], one is the cause of one only. Therefore, it is necessary to postulate—beyond this deformed concatenation—some first essential cause which perpetuates it. The deformation, then, is due to the deformed cause, but the continual

uniformity of this deformity will be due to a cause outside this concatenation. And thus, if there is a process in incidentally ordered causes, there will still be a terminal point in some first essential cause upon which all the incidentally ordered causes depend.

In this way we avoid begging the question as regards a terminus and order of essential causes.

56 Now for the second objection raised against the aforesaid argument, viz. that it proceeds from something contingent, scil. "Something other than God exists." The philosophers would say that this is something necessary because of the essential order that holds between the cause and what it produces.

But I say, first, that even though it be contingent with reference to God, it is nevertheless most evident, so that anyone who would deny the existence of some being which is not eternal needs senses and punishment. And therefore, from what is contingent in this way we can establish something necessary, for from the contingent something necessary follows, but not vice versa.

57 Also, I say that although things other than God are actually contingent as regards their actual existence, this is not true with regard to potential existence. Wherefore, those things which are said to be contingent with reference to actual existence are necessary with respect to potential existence. Thus, though "Man exists" is contingent, "It is possible for man to exist" is necessary, because it does not include a contradiction as regards existence. For, for something other than God to be possible, then, is necessary. Being is divided into what must exist and what can but need not be. And just as necessity is of the very essence or constitution of what must be, so possibility is of the very essence of what can but need not be. Therefore, let the former argument be couched in terms of possible being and the propositions will become necessary. Thus: It is possible that something other than God exist which neither exists of itself (for then it would not be possible being) nor exists by reason of nothing. Therefore, it can exist by reason of another. Either this other can both exist and act in virtue of itself and not in virtue of another, or it cannot do so. If it can, then it can be the first cause, and if it can exist, it does exist—as was proved above. If it cannot [both be and act independently of every other thing] and there is no infinite regress, then at some point we end up [with a first cause].

58 To the other objection (viz. that whenever an argument proceeds by way of a demonstration of simple fact, a converse demonstration of the reasoned fact can be constructed), one must say that such is not always true, because when we argue from the effect to the existence of a cause our argument may merely prove that the latter is a necessary condition rather than a sufficient reason for the effect. But it is only when the argument from effect to cause establishes the latter as a sufficient reason that the above principle [of converse demonstration] holds good.

59 And so we show from efficiency, to begin with, that something which is first exists, for—as we have made clear—something exists which makes all possible things possible. But that which makes all possibles possible cannot fail to exist of itself, for otherwise it would be from nothing. Therefore, it must needs be actually self–existent. And so our thesis is proved.

2. The Argument from Finality

60 That something first exists is established secondly from finality. Something is suited by its very nature to be an end. Hence it so functions either in virtue of itself or in virtue of another. If the first be the case, we have something which is first; if it functions as an end only in virtue of another then this other is suited by its very nature to be an end, and since there is no infinite regress, we arrive at some end which is first. This is the argument of the Philosopher in Metaphysics, Bk. II and Bk. XII about the most perfect good, and it is also the argument of Augustine in On the Trinity, Bk. VIII, chapter three: "Consider this good and that good, abstract from the 'this' and the 'that,' and consider, if you can, simply the good itself, and thus you will see God, who is not good by reason of some other good but is the goodness of all that is good."

[3. The Argument from Eminent Perfection]

61 The third way is that of eminence. Some good is exceeded in perfection, or is able to be exceeded if you prefer to argue from possibility. Therefore, there is something which exceeds or is able to exceed something else in perfection. The latter either is or is not able to be exceeded or is actually exceeded in perfection by something else. If it is not, then it is first in the order of eminence, if it is not first and there is no regress ad infinitum, then we argue the same as before.

62 And so we show that something is first in three ways, first in the order of efficiency, first in the order of eminence and first in the order of ends.

And this triple "first" is one and the same because the first efficient cause is fully actualized, while the most eminent is the best of things. But what is fully actualized is also the best, with no mixture of evil or potentiality. Then too, the first efficient cause does not act for the sake of anything other than itself, for if it did, this other would be better than it. Consequently, it is the ultimate end, and hence first in the order of ends. The same thing, then, enjoys [a triple primacy].

63 Before establishing that some being is infinite, we prove God is his own knowledge, for if his knowledge were not his nature but something accidental to it, then as the first efficient cause of everything, he would produce his knowledge. But God acts with knowledge; hence he would have to know about this knowledge beforehand. About this prior knowledge we inquire as before. Either there will be an infinite regress before something is known—and then nothing will be known—(or we admit finally that God is his own knowledge].

B. Proof of the Infinity of God

64 I turn now from these things to the thesis to be proved and declare that this most eminent being, which is both the ultimate and as well as the first efficient cause, is infinite.

65 The first proof of this makes use of the notion of efficiency as employed by the Philosopher in Bk. VIII of the Physics where he argues that, inasmuch as the first mover moves for an infinite time, it follows that he has infinite power.

66 Of course you may object to this argument on two grounds: first, the antecedent as a matter of fact is not true, since motion will not continue forever.

67 Furthermore, the inference itself seems to be invalid, since, according to the mind of the Philosopher, a body like the sun, though its power is finite, will continue to move things for an infinite time—and as a matter of fact, it could move things for an infinite period.

68 For these reasons, some reword the argument in this fashion. Where a cause produces its effects in virtue of itself alone, it has in its power at once all the effects which are produced in succession, for such an agent cannot receive power to act from anything other than itself, and hence it holds within its power at one and the same time all the effects it will eventually produce. The first efficient cause acts in virtue of itself and hence holds in its power at one and the same time all the effects which are successively produced, and these are potentially infinite. But this is to have infinite power. Now this is not, they say, the case with the sun, since it acts in virtue of something other than itself, and consequently it does hold in its power at one and the same time all of the effects it will eventually produce.

69 Also, were the first mover to move for an infinite period of time, it could produce eventually an infinity of things, because with each movement it could produce something and this by reason of itself alone. But to possess in itself an ability to produce an infinity of things is to possess infinite power.

70 These reasons, however, are not conclusive because an effect does not become more perfect because it continues to exist for more than a moment. Whiteness which lasts for a hundred years, for instance, is not more perfect than whiteness which lasts for a day. In like manner, a cause does not become more perfect because it produces its effect repeatedly instead of once. The same strength that enables something to move once a day, will enable it to move for an infinite period of time. All that is established, consequently, is the eternity of the cause, but from this one cannot infer its infinity.

71 Furthermore, to produce several individuals of the same species successively is not a matter of any greater perfection than to produce one individual at one time. Something hot [like the sun], for example, does not become more perfect by making several things hot over a period of time than it was when making one thing hot. But this infinity of things which are produced by means of motion concerns things which are only individually, and not specifically, distinct. Consequently, its production implies no greater perfection [in the cause] than does the production of a single individual.

72 Still one must say that the argument of the Philosopher is valid, for even though the antecedent is false if it is understood of what is actually the case, the antecedent is true if you take it of what could be the case, without averting to whether it is or not. For if the first mover could move for an infinite period of time and it does not derive this power

from anything other than itself, then it possesses such power of itself. And from this follows the further conclusion that it is of infinite power, so that the inference is valid. The proof lies in this. Whenever numerical plurality in one extreme requires a greater perfection in the other extreme, where the plurality of the one is infinite, the perfection of the other is infinite. For example, if to carry ten objects requires more strength than to carry one, then to carry an infinite number requires infinite strength. To produce several things at one time, however, requires more power than to produce but one; therefore, to produce an infinity requires infinite power. But the first mover, so far as it itself is concerned, could produce an infinity at one time, as I shall prove. Therefore, in itself it will be of infinite power.—Proof of the assumption: It is clear that the first efficient cause has power as a remote cause to cause an infinity at once, if such an infinity were able to be produced. But if the proximate causes by which things are produced successively all existed at the same time as the remote first cause, they could produce an infinity at once. Since the power of the first efficient cause, however, includes all the formal powers of the intermediary causes which are potentially infinite, and it possesses all of the causalities of all intermediary causes in an even more perfect way than if they were actualized, as will be proved, it follows that the first efficient cause, so far as it itself is concerned, has power to produce an actual infinity. Proof of the assumption: It is clear that the first cause possesses the causality of the proximate cause more perfectly than the latter, because this latter has its causality only in virtue of the first cause. Similarly, the second cause possesses the causality of the third cause more perfectly than the latter, since the third cause receives its causality from the second, and so on down to the lowest cause. Consequently, the first cause possesses more perfectly the causalities of the intermediary causes, from first to last, than they do themselves.

73 Another proof of the implication is this. It is not that the causality of the production is more perfect that the second cause is needed to work with the first cause. (Proof: if it were for the sake of a more perfect causality that several causes are needed to produce a given effect, then the effect produced by the lot would be more perfect than the effect produced by one cause; now it is the effect furthest removed [from the first cause] that needs all the causes, whereas the nearest effect needs only the first cause. But since the more remote effect is less perfect than the proximate effect, it follows that it is not because of any weakness in its causality that the first cause requires the cooperation of a second cause.) Hence, if the first cause could produce an actual infinity of effects provided only that all of the infinitely numerous intermediary causes were actualized, then it follows that so far as the first cause itself is concerned, it could produce an

infinity, and consequently, it will be infinitely powerful.

74 That is why the philosophers wished to say that the reason a second cause was needed to cooperate with the first cause was not because of any deficiency as regards causality, but it was to explain how an imperfect effect could be produced. For they thought that it was only through the intervention of some intermediary cause that an imperfect effect could be produced by a perfect first cause.

75 Using this way of efficiency, some add as a further proof of our thesis that inasmuch as the first being is able to create, it must have infinite power. They show that this follows because there is an infinite distance between contradictories which nothing short of an infinite power can bridge. Hence, since to create is to make something from nothing, it follows that if the first efficient cause can create, its power is infinite.

76 This argument, however, has no force.

First, it assumes that there is a creation—which is something we take on faith—and consequently, it is not a demonstration.

Secondly, between contradictories there is the least of all "distance," for no matter how little something departs from the one extreme, it immediately comes under the other. Hence there is the least latitude or distance here, although virtually speaking the distance between contradictories is greatest because this minimal distance between them establishes the "distance" and opposition between all other extremes.

77 What is more, the argument has another defect inasmuch as distance can be understood to be infinite in two ways. Either the distance in itself is infinite in the sense that it lacks limits as would be the case if one has an endless line, or the distance is infinite by reason of one of the extremes. We speak of a creature being infinitely distant from God, for instance. This is only because the one extreme is infinite. And even if we assumed the existence of the most perfect creature possible, between such a creature and God there would still be an infinite distance in the second sense. And it is in just this sense that "distance" between something and nothing or between affirmation and negation is to be understood. Consequently, negation is no more distant from affirmation than is the affirmation itself, and therefore whatever is able to make the affirmation is able to bridge the distance. Consequently, the argument is not conclusive.

A TREATISE ON GOD AS FIRST PRINCIPLE

78 The second main argument for infinity stems from divine knowledge. As was said above, whenever numerical plurality implies the presence of greater perfection, then an infinite number implies the presence of infinite perfection. Knowledge whereby several things are known distinctly is more perfect than knowledge whereby only one such is known, as I shall prove. Hence, knowledge of an actual infinity requires infinite perfection. Now the first intelligent and efficient cause with a single intellection knows an infinity of things actually and distinctly, as I shall show. Therefore, it is actually of infinite perfection.

79 Proof of the first assumption: To know each object distinctly requires some perfection, hence to know several objects in this way is something more perfect. If then there is a single intellection which actually contains the knowledge of them all, it will be of greater perfection than would be the knowledge of only one.

Proof of the second assumption, that God's knowledge has to do with an actual infinity, like an infinity of figures and numbers: Wherever you have a potential infinity, if all its members were to exist at the same time, you would have an actual infinity. This is clear if you consider the consequences of any alternate hypothesis. Consider the intelligibles which we know by thinking of one after another. They are potentially infinite and they are all actually known by God, because he knows whatever can be. Hence, he knows an actual infinity.

80 The third argument for infinity is drawn from the fact that the divine essence itself serves as the [principle or] reason why God knows. For just as knowledge wherein several things are grasped distinctly is more perfect than that wherein but one is known, so also is the principle for knowing several things more perfect than is a principle for knowing only one of them. And an essence which represents several things distinctly will be more perfect than one which represents but one. But the divine essence represents an infinity of things distinctly, and consequently, its power of representation is infinite. Therefore the [essence itself] is infinite.

81 What is more, the reason this is so lies not merely in the ability of [the essence] to make all things known distinctly but because it produces a clear vision of a thing like a stone. If something is the precise effect of some cause, and nevertheless something else can produce the same effect in even more perfect fashion, the proper cause cannot add anything to the perfection of the latter. If something be the precise cause of a for instance,

and if b causes the same effect even more perfectly, then it is impossible that a should add anything to b. For were there any perfection to be added, it would be because b lacked some perfection needed to produce the effect in question, since it is precisely this effect that a's power is adequate to achieve. Any object, however, by its very nature is fitted to be the precise and proper cause of an [intuition or] vision of itself. It is impossible, then, that such a vision be achieved in an even more perfect manner unless it be by reason of something to which nothing in the way of perfection could be added. But such a vision is had even more perfectly by reason of the divine essence, so that neither a stone, nor any other essence, could add anything to the perfection of the divine essence. But anything of this kind is infinite. Therefore, etc.

82 The fourth argument for infinity is derived from the fact that God is an end. Our will can love a good that exceeds that of any finite good. This we know, first, because our intellect can know such a good, and also because our will is inclined to seek an infinite good, for it delights in evoking such an act of love, which would not be the case if it were not inclined to do so. If the ultimate end were not an infinite good, however, the will would not be inclined towards, nor seek, an infinite good. Proof: It is incompatible with the very notion of an ultimate end that there be any good greater than it, as we have shown [Cf. par. 60]. For then it could either exist of itself, or in virtue of another, neither of which can be assumed to be the case. If the ultimate end, then, were finite and not infinite, it would be impossible for any good to be infinite. And if this were so, the will could neither love the infinite nor be inclined towards it, because it has no inclination towards the opposite of its object.

83 The fifth argument for infinity is based on the eminence [of God]. Anything to which infinity is not repugnant, is not simply perfect unless it is infinite. For instance, if the tenth degree of some perfection is not repugnant to a certain thing, then it is not simply perfect unless it possesses the tenth degree. But to being qua being infinity is not repugnant, as will be proved. Therefore, the most eminent and most perfect being will be infinite.

84 Proof of the assumption: If "infinite" were repugnant to "being," then the repugnance would either be formal, like "man" and "not—man," or virtual, like "man" and "not—risible." The first is not the case, for formal repugnance stems from the meaning of the terms. But as Avicenna teaches in Bk. I of the Metaphysics, the meaning and notion of "being" cannot be made any clearer. The concept of "infinite" is also clear, because the

infinite is that which cannot be surpassed. But there is no contradiction between these notions, for there is no contradiction that something be a being and that it cannot be surpassed. Neither is there any virtual repugnance, for the primary attributes of "being" such as "true," and "good" and such like, are most evidently characteristic of being. But this is not the case with "infinite," for "being" does not of itself include "infinite" as a coextensive attribute. Consequently, "being is infinite" is not a primary truth unless you add in disjunction its opposite [viz. "being is either infinite or finite"].

85 Also since an amount of power is of greater perfection than an amount of mass, and since infinity is not repugnant to the latter, then neither is it opposed to the former.

86 Another proof of the same point is this. Any faculty naturally perceives any lack of harmony in its object, and it will not naturally put up with it or be content with it. If then "infinite" were something that contradicted "being," our mind would be naturally repelled by "infinite being" as something which includes a contradiction. But this is false, for our mind rather than finding any contradiction discovers its rest therein.

IV. To the Arguments at the Beginning of the First Question (par. 1–6)

87 Consider the first argument, where it is said that if one of the contraries were infinite, it would be incompatible with anything other than itself. It must be admitted that this would be true if we were dealing with an agent that was necessitated by its nature to act, as is clear from the case cited about the sun. It is not true, however, if that which is either virtually or formally contrary turns out to be an agent which is not necessitated in this way. Hence, if God acted by a necessity of his nature, it would not be possible for evil to occur, for it is virtually contrary to himself and formally contrary to what he causes, viz. the good of the universe.

88 You may object that the philosophers assumed that God and the first good acted out of necessity in their nature, and still they admitted that evil could occur in the world.

To this I reply that they could not save the fact that evil occurs contingently or that anything occurs contingently, on the assumption that God acts by a necessity of his nature. For if God produced the first effect in such a way, since the latter could only in turn produce something in virtue of the first [being] by which it was produced, it follows that this next effect is also produced by a necessity of nature, and so on down [through the hierarchy of celestial causes] to the fact of my sitting now, which would also need to be produced by a necessity of nature.

89 Still the philosophers could maintain that evil occurred in the world by a necessity of nature, since they claimed that God moved one series of causes which terminated in the eduction of the form and another series which brought about the superabundance of matter. That the body of an animal is an organism results from the first series, whereas that it has too many members is a consequence of the second. And so it happens that the animal turns out to be a freak. Yet this does not happen contingently, because if the one cause acts necessarily, so the other impedes its action necessarily. There is no alternative good, however, to evil of this kind, for it was a matter of necessity that these other causes impede the action since they are the stronger.

90 But you may say that although the Philosopher assumed that a heavenly body was necessarily produced by God, he still held that such a body, like the sun, had different movements, and according to its proximity or distance from us it could cause events contingently, and in consequence, some things do occur contingently.

I claim this does not follow. For while he could admit that even though God acts of necessity by reason of the way explained above, it could be that something does not exist forever, and to that extent, has contingent existence. But he could not consistently hold that the thing occurred contingently [i.e. that it need not have occurred at the time it did] as the reason above proves [Cf. par. 88].

91 [To Arg. II] The second main argument should be answered by denying the validity of the inference. And as for the proof wherein it is claimed that just as two bodies cannot coexist in one place because of their opposed dimensions, so neither can two spirits because of their opposed actualizations, it should be pointed out that there is no parallel between the two. The reason this holds in regard to bodies is that one body fills a place to the full extent that place can be filled. Similarly, the reason two opposed forms cannot coexist in matter is that matter is perfected by one to the extent of its capacity. But beings are not so proportioned that one being takes up all the room so that there cannot be more than one.

92 As for the other proof of the inference, I say again that there is no parallel. If one assumed that another body coexisted with an infinite body, there would be an opposition

83

viz. that there would be something both infinite and finite. But if a finite spirit is assumed to coexist with an infinite spirit such an opposition does not follow, because when the finite spirit is present with the infinite, there is no one thing which results that is of greater perfection than is the infinite spirit itself, for the latter's perfection stems from itself whereas the other's is derived from another.

93 [To Arg. III] As for the other argument, we must point out that it does not follow. Neither is the manner of arguing valid except for what is finite. It is not valid as regards the infinite, as for example, when it is assumed that whereabouts is infinite and a body is infinite. For then it does not follow "This body is in this place in such a way that it is in no other, therefore it is finite as to its whereabouts." Or, "Motion is at this time so that it is not at another, therefore it is finite in time" does not follow either according to the view of the Philosopher, who assumed that motion was perpetual. And so too it does not hold for what they try to prove, viz. "God is just this essence in such a way that he is no other, therefore he is finite." What does indeed follow is that he is not numerically infinite, but it does not follow that he is not intensively infinite.

94 [To Arg. IV] As for the next, we must insist that the Philosopher did not say that if an infinite power were to move things, it would do so in an instant. What he intended to prove there was that infinite power does not reside in any magnitude, because if it did it would move things instantaneously. And the reason is this: an infinite power, if it were to move things according to the utmost of its power and by a necessity of nature, would move them instantaneously (Proof: if it were to move things only over a period of time, then some other finite power could be increased to a point where it could move an equal amount in an equal period of time, and thus the two powers, each doing the utmost it could do, would be equal). If an infinite power were to reside in some body, however, it would be a power to move, since it is clear enough from the context that the Philosopher there is speaking about a power which is divided up according to the divisions of a body so that the greater power resides in what is larger and in any part thereof it is only there in part. And what is more, since a body can be divided and can differ as to the position of its parts, it is the whole that is needed to produce movement. And consequently [if it were infinite] it would move things and do so instantaneously [which is a contradiction]. Now although we too postulate an infinite power, we do not claim that it moves things to the utmost of its ability. Hence it does not follow that it moves things in an instant. What does indeed follow is that it could act instantaneously and could transfer a body from one place to another in an instant, but this is not to "move" in the proper meaning of the word.

Neither would there be any motion in such a case.

95 The Philosopher, you may object, claimed the first mover acted of necessity and to the utmost of its ability, and he proves it to be of infinite power. Still it does not follow that it moves instantaneously, for he admits that the heavens move in time.—I say that if the Philosopher were to postulate that the first mover acts necessarily, he cannot also assume that anything is moved immediately; motion can only occur through the intervention of some finite cause. With this Averroes agrees in Bk. XII of the Metaphysics, where he says that the heavens have a double motor cause, one which exists apart and guarantees the perpetuity of the movement, and another which is captivated by the former. But it is only the combination of the two that allows for temporal movement. Here is the complete list of proper names occurring in this work:

Anselm
Aristotle
Augustine
Averroes
Avicenna
Heracliteans
Moses
Plato
Proslogion.

CPSIA information can be obtained
at www.ICGtesting.com
Printed in the USA
BVHW012257130822
644551BV00011B/390

9 781162 650 7